Embellished Embroidery Kit

Pauline Brown

Watson - Guptill Publications/New York

A QUARTO BOOK

Copyright © 1998 Quarto Inc.

First published in 1998 in the United States
by Watson-Guptill Publications Inc.,
a division of BPI Communications, Inc.,
1515 Broadway, New York, N.Y. 10036

All rights reserved. No part of this publication may be reproduced
or used in any form or by any means—graphic, electronic, or mechanical,
including photocopying, recording, taping, or information storage and
retrieval systems—without written permission of the publisher.

ISBN 0-8230-1595-5

This book was designed and produced by
Quarto Publishing plc
The Old Brewery
6 Blundell Street
London N7 9BH

Project editor *Anne Hildyard*
Copy editor *Eleanor van Zandt*
Art editor *Sally Bond*
Assistant art editor *Sue Megginson*
Designer *Karin Skånberg*
Illustrator *Kate Simunek*
Index *Dorothy Frame*
Photographer *Colin Bowling*
Picture researchers *Anne Hildyard, Gill Metcalf*
Art director *Moira Clinch*
Assistant art director *Penny Cobb*
Publisher *Marion Hasson*

Typeset by Central Southern Typesetters, Eastbourne, UK
Manufactured by Regent Publishing Services Ltd, Hong Kong
Printed by Winner Offset Printing Factory Ltd, Hong Kong

ACKNOWLEDGMENTS

Quarto would like to thank the following who kindly supplied
projects for this book

Ribbon Hair Slide: *Susie Johns*
Victorian Valentine Pincushion: *Lucinda Ganderton*
Appliqué Folk Art Picture: *Lucinda Ganderton*
Patchwork and Appliqué Pillowcase: *Cheryl Owen*
Wildflower Party Bolero: *Isabel Stanley*
Wedding Ring Pillow, Art Deco Brooch and Autumn Sampler:
*Gay Bowles Sales Inc., Mill Hill, 3930 Enterprise Drive, PO Box 1060,
Janesville, WI 53547-1060 USA*

Contents

INTRODUCTION 4

EQUIPMENT AND MATERIALS 5
TRANSFERRING THE DESIGN TO FABRIC 10
STITCHES 12

KIT COMPONENTS—HOW TO USE 15

Kit Projects
BEADED TRINKET BOX 16
ELEGANT EVENING BAG 18
RIBBON HAIR SLIDE 20

Other Projects
SPARKLY EVENING PURSE 22
WILDFLOWER PARTY BOLERO 24
WEDDING RING PILLOW 26
ART DECO BROOCH 28
APPLIQUE FOLK ART PICTURE 30
JEWELED PICTURE FRAME 32
VICTORIAN PINCUSHION 34
APPLIQUE PATCHWORK PILLOWCASE 36
AUTUMN SAMPLER 38

GALLERY 40

TEMPLATES 44

INDEX 48

Introduction

Embroidery is one of the most versatile of the decorative arts. Not only is there a wealth of stitches to choose from, but ribbons and laces, buttons and bows, beads and sequins, and tassels and cords, as well as appliquéd motifs, can all be incorporated to give a luxurious effect.

Throughout the centuries, European and American craftsmen and women have decorated their homes and garments with stitchery, adding appliqué, lace, sequins, and beads to stunning effect. We are all familiar with portraits of the Elizabethans and early Stuarts in their elaborate finery—the jeweled bodices, blackwork sleeves, and heavy, brocaded skirts. Men's clothing was almost equally rich, with ruffs, collars, and cuffs made of luxurious lace a common sight at court.

In the eighteenth century, more delicate forms of decoration were popular. Men's waistcoats were often embroidered with exquisitely worked floral designs, and before printed fabrics were developed, women's dresses were patterned with stitchery. In the houses of the rich, soft furnishings were highly regarded as status symbols—heavily embroidered and tasseled bed-hangings and covers were often the centerpiece of the bedchamber, and chairs were upholstered with needlepoint designs of great intricacy.

The nineteenth century brought a revolution in the lives of the growing middle classes; ladies were educated in social skills, which included needlework of all types. This was the time when "art and craft" work became extremely popular, and Victorian parlors would be furnished with beadwork pictures and stools, tasseled covers, and lace-edged cushions.

During our own century fashions have changed radically. The elaborately decorated costumes of the Edwardian era gave way in the twenties and thirties to a vogue for beaded and fringed "flapper" dresses. The necessary economizing during the Second World War

Diana Dolman Venice I & II
Rich embroidery in gold and silver with sparkling blue beads.

and the postwar period resulted in much plainer fashions and furnishings with little decoration. It is only in the past twenty or thirty years that people have again become interested in using embroidery for its wonderful decorative textures and patterns. Nowadays international fashion designers use beads, sequins, and free-standing appliqué motifs to accentuate or even cover their garments, and interior decorators attach cords and tassels to cushions, slipcovers, and draperies (curtains).

Of course, this love of elaborate decoration is not confined to Western cultures. In many countries of the world, beautifully embroidered costumes are still worn at festivals and important occasions such as weddings. The women in places as far apart as the Middle East and Thailand decorate their headdresses with coins, shells, and tassels. In India and Pakistan, there is a tradition of using "shisha" mirrors surrounded with embroidery, and in many African countries, elaborate beadwork is used to decorate both clothes and useful articles.

We can take ideas for embellishing our craftwork from all these sources. For purely decorative articles, there are few limitations as to materials or techniques; for dress embroidery, the traditional methods of stitchery, beading, and appliqué are still most suitable.

All the techniques described in this book can be adapted or modified for use in your own creative projects. With a little practice you will be able to produce individual handmade gifts, attractive keepsakes, sophisticated garments, or contemporary items, such as cushions and picture frames, for your home.

Equipment and Materials

Much of the equipment needed for embellishing the projects in this book is readily available; in fact, most people will already have in their workbox a selection of needles, pins, scissors, and threads.

EQUIPMENT

Needles

It is important to choose the correct needle for the job—one that suits the technique, the type of fabric, and the thickness of the yarn or thread. A good guide is to select one through which the yarn can be threaded easily and that pierces the fabric comfortably. Embroidery (or crewel) needles are available in sizes 1–10 and have elongated eyes. These take most types of embroidery thread. Chenille needles have larger eyes and come in sizes 13–24, which makes them a good choice for thicker threads and for ribbon embroidery. Beading needles are the longest and finest and are essential for tiny beads, although for beads with larger holes a fine embroidery needle can be used. Tapestry needles, which come in sizes 13–26, have blunt points and are used for counted-thread techniques, such as cross stitch, in which it is important not to split the fabric threads. Bodkins (threading needles) are used for threading cords and elastic through casing.

A selection of needles in various sizes for different sewing tasks. They are always kept threaded through a piece of fabric for safety.

EMBELLISHED EMBROIDERY KIT

Frames and hoops

For best results, it is always a good idea to work embroidery in a frame or hoop. The frame will support the fabric, keep the work smooth, and make it simple to maintain an even tension when stitching. To prepare the fabric, press it carefully, and back it, if the fabric is thin or needs support, by basting (tacking) the two fabrics together, keeping the warp and woof (weft) running at right angles to one another.

Embroidery hoops

Embroidery hoops (ring frames) are essential to achieve the best results. Using a hoop ensures that the fabric will remain clean and uncrumpled and that the tension of the stitches will be even. Hoops come in wood or metal and may be bound to protect delicate fabrics.

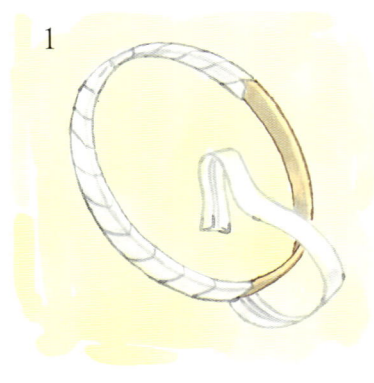

Embroidery hoops (or ring frames) are available in various sizes and are suitable for most small projects if the design fits within the frame. Bind the inner ring with bias binding to provide a good grip and protect delicate fabrics (see fig. 1).

To mount the fabric, adjust the screw of the outer ring so that it fits loosely over the inner ring. Place the fabric, with the design centered, over the inner ring (see fig. 2) and press the outer ring down, making sure that the fabric is straight and taut. Secure by tightening the screw.

Stretcher frames

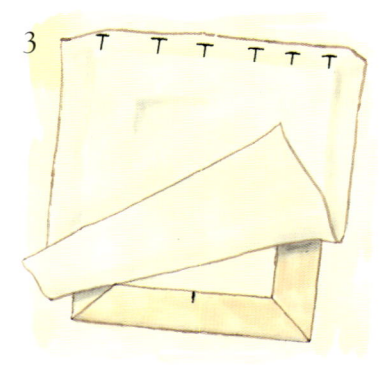

For a project that is too large to fit in a hoop, a stretcher frame (or even a suitably sized old picture frame), consisting of four lengths of soft wood with mitered corners, is a good alternative. Mark the center of each inner edge of the frame, and make corresponding marks on the fabric. Starting at the top edge, align the center marks and secure with a thumbtack (drawing pin). Pin at ½-inch/1.5-cm intervals, working toward the corners. Fasten the bottom edge in the same way, stretching the fabric so that it is straight and taut (see fig. 3).

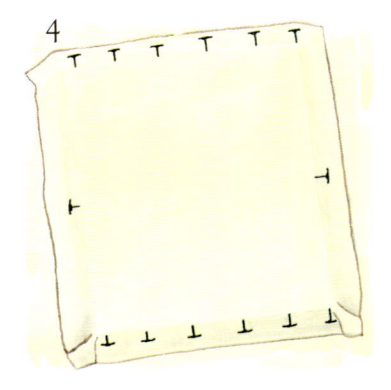

Attach the other two sides by pinning the center points (see fig. 4) and continuing toward the corners, pinning first one side then the other to maintain an even tension.

EQUIPMENT AND MATERIALS

Fabric markers

A variety of fabric markers is available, such as dressmaker's chalk and pencils, and water-soluble and fade-away pens. These should be pressed down very lightly, so that the marks do not show when the embroidery is complete.

Other equipment

Two pairs of **scissors** are needed for embroidery—a small pair for trimming threads and for intricate tasks, and a larger pair for cutting out fabric.

Dressmaker's pins are useful for holding layers of fabric in place and for holding beads and sequins in decorative projects such as the traditional Victorian-style pincushion. A **tape measure** is essential, whereas the use of a **thimble** is a matter of personal choice.

Design equipment

Most of the basic design equipment for the projects in this book will be readily at hand. Pencils, ruler, sketchpad, and tracing paper are all that are needed, though you may find that crayons, felt-tip markers, or colored pencils will help you to visualize your ideas more fully.

Some drawing aids, such as a compass for drawing circles, a right-angled triangle (T-square, or set square) for geometric designs, and a protractor for measuring angles, can be bought as the need arises. Adhesives, including all-purpose adhesive, fabric glue, and various tapes such as masking tape and transparent (sticky) tape, are useful additions to your workbox.

Clockwise from bottom left: adhesive, metal ruler, pins, thimble, compass, small scissors, sketch pad, felt-tip marker, crayon, tape measure, masking tape, transparent (sticky) tape, protractor, large scissors.

EMBELLISHED EMBROIDERY KIT

MATERIALS

Threads

A large number of different threads and yarns are available today, ranging from conventional embroidery threads to knitting and crochet yarns, ribbons, and cords. For dressmaking and for general sewing, by hand or machine, cotton or cotton-covered polyester thread is used. Special cotton basting (tacking) thread is soft and easily removed. For most embroidery projects, stranded cotton embroidery floss is a good choice, as the six strands can be divided to make different thicknesses. Embroidery wools, such as crewel, Persian, and tapestry wool, although manufactured primarily for needlepoint, are also useful for doing surface embroidery on coarsely woven fabric and making interesting cords, tassels, and trimmings.

Synthetic metallic threads come in various thicknesses, types, and colors, not only silver and gold, but also rich jewel shades which can add a touch of luxury to an article. Synthetic metallic threads have an advantage over pure metal threads in that they can usually be washed or dry-cleaned.

Fabrics

Your choice of fabric will depend not only on the color, texture, and weight, but also on its suitability for the project at hand. Almost any fabric can be used for purely decorative articles, whereas garments and household items may require a fabric that can be laundered or dry-cleaned. In addition, you should choose a fabric that suits the technique you want to use, and consider whether its thickness and handling characteristics are correct for the scale of the article. For counted-thread projects—for example, samplers using such techniques as counted cross stitch, Hardanger embroidery, and pulled work—an evenly woven fabric is essential. If you decide to use cotton fabrics in a project, it is a good idea to prewash and iron the fabric before cutting it out.

Batting (wadding), usually made of synthetic fibers, is essential for padding quilted items, creating slightly raised effects, and stuffing three-dimensional shapes. It comes in several thicknesses, and your choice will depend not only on scale but also on the desired effect.

Non-woven iron-on or sew-in interfacings, designed for dressmaking, are ideal for stiffening fabrics and for backing projects. Transfer bonding web (Bondaweb), which comes with a paper backing, is very useful for fusing fabrics together.

Embellishments

Decorative elements such as beads, sequins, and jewels give a lavish, often theatrical, effect when stitched to a piece of embroidery as additional embellishments. They are available in myriad colors, shapes, and sizes. Your choice will depend not only on the aesthetic aspect of the design but also on the scale of the embroidery project. They can be massed together, scattered randomly, or used to accentuate certain areas; and their eye-catching quality will cause them to dominate the area where they are placed.

Beads come in many forms and may be made of glass, china, wood, or plastic. Rocaille beads are round and bugles are long, but others are faceted, pendant, or lozenge-shaped. **Sequins**, with their faceted shape, and flat spangles are usually round with a central hole, but some specialty shops carry sequins in the form of flowers, leaves, stars, hearts, and geometric shapes. **Fake jewels**, specially produced for attaching to fabric, come with flat undersides and often have holes that allow them to be stitched to the background fabric. Those without holes must be secured with glue or covering stitches.

Ribbon, lace edging, and braid have been used as dress decoration for centuries. They can be used to trim or accentuate an edge and can also be arranged in geometric patterns. Sewing ribbon, lace, or braid appliqué in straight lines is simple to do, especially by machine, as there are no raw edges to contend with. For curved designs or for added fullness, the material will need to be slightly gathered before attaching.

Ribbons are available in different widths and fabrics, from narrow silk ribbon, suitable for embroidery, to heavy, wide grosgrain and velvet. Indeed, ribbon embroidery has seen such a revival in recent years that narrow-width ribbons are now readily available specifically for this purpose. **Lace** for appliqué or edging can be cut from material purchased from a fabric store.

Cords, plaits, and tassels provide a pleasing finishing touch to many articles. These can be bought readymade, or you can make your own from threads that complement those used in the embroidery. Simple three-, four-, or five-strand **plaits** make attractive trimmings, and **cords** can be twisted in several colors. **Tassels** can range from simple types to those with elaborate headings and skirts.

EMBELLISHED EMBROIDERY KIT

Transferring the Design to Fabric

Having selected or worked out a design for a project, you will need to transfer the image to the fabric. There are several methods, suitable for different fabrics and techniques and for designs of different levels of complexity.

Fabric markers

A number of specially produced fabric pens and pencils are available for marking a design onto fabric. Your choice will depend not only on the technique and fabric but also on the intricacy of the design. Whichever type you select, mark the design as lightly as possible, so that the marks will not show once the final stitching has been done.

Dressmaker's chalk, sharpened to a fine edge, is useful for large-scale designs, though dressmaker's chalk pens will give better definition. Water-soluble and fade-away pens are an option for light-colored fabrics, and a hard pencil is suitable for smooth, fine materials.

Crayons, felt-tip marker, dressmaker's chalk, white marker pencil, T-square (set square).

TRANSFERRING THE DESIGN

Trace and baste (tacking)

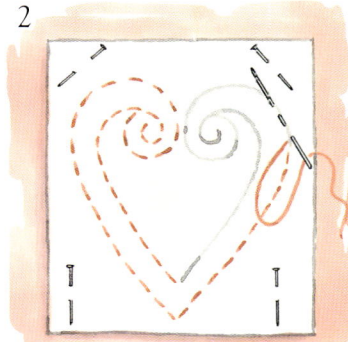

This method is best for simple or bold designs with little detail. Trace the design and pin the tracing to the fabric. Starting with a knot and a backstitch, work small running stitches along the marked lines, through both layers (see fig. 2).

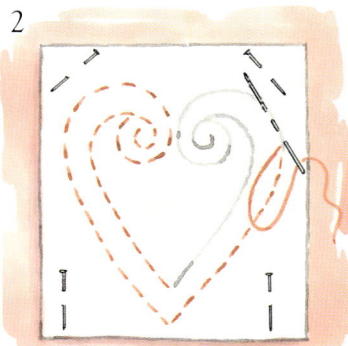

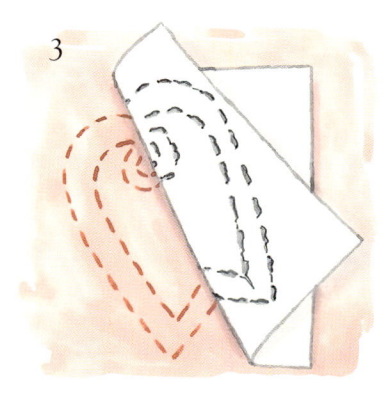

Fasten off with a double backstitch. Gently tear away the tracing paper to reveal the basted (tacked) line (see fig. 3), which should be removed as the embroidery progresses.

Working from a chart

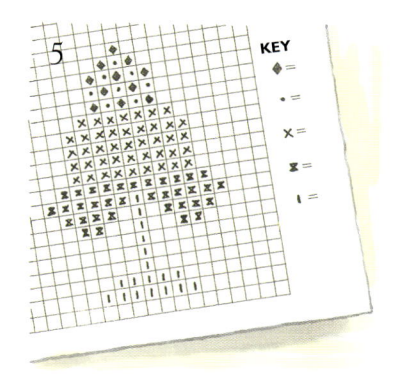

Designs for counted-thread embroidery are usually worked out on box charts, with each square corresponding to a single stitch. Symbols shown on a key denoting different colors or stitches are used to recreate the design on the fabric (see fig. 5). The center of the area of fabric where the design is to be placed is marked with two intersecting lines of basting (tacking).

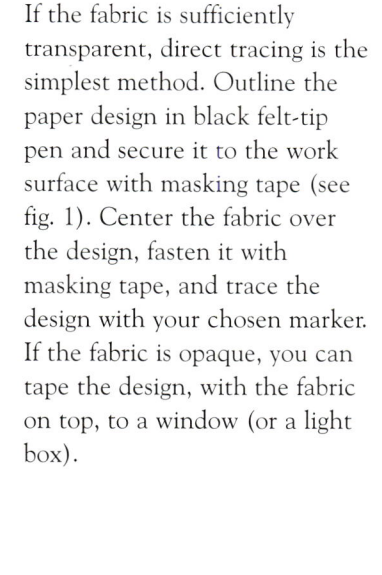

Direct tracing

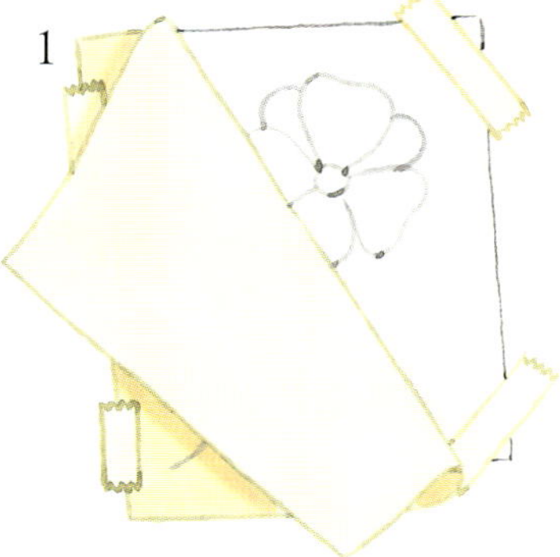

If the fabric is sufficiently transparent, direct tracing is the simplest method. Outline the paper design in black felt-tip pen and secure it to the work surface with masking tape (see fig. 1). Center the fabric over the design, fasten it with masking tape, and trace the design with your chosen marker. If the fabric is opaque, you can tape the design, with the fabric on top, to a window (or a light box).

Dressmaker's carbon

This comes in several colors and is used in the same way as ordinary carbon paper. Test the effect before beginning, and use a dotted line if a continuous line will be too heavy. Tape the fabric to the work surface, with the carbon paper, colored side down, on top. Then tape the traced design on top of both carbon and fabric and, using a ballpoint pen, draw over the marked lines, pressing firmly (see fig. 4).

11

EMBELLISHED EMBROIDERY KIT

Stitches

Surface stitches are the basis of embellished embroidery, enabling you to create different effects and techniques. Stitches can be grouped in a number of ways, to make lines, form circles or create pattern. They can be adapted and modified to produce different effects by altering scale and direction or working with different thicknesses and types of yarn. Stitches can be very effective when combined with other embellishments, such as appliqué.

Backstitch

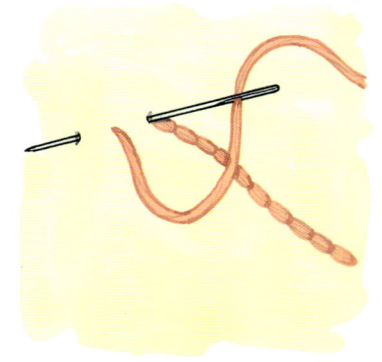

One of the basic stitches of embroidery, backstitch produces an unbroken line, similar to machine-stitching. It can be used as an outline or to sew two fabrics together.

Working from right to left, bring the needle out on the stitching line a short distance from the starting point, and take a small stitch back to the starting point. Bring the needle out ahead of the first stitch and repeat.

Fly stitch

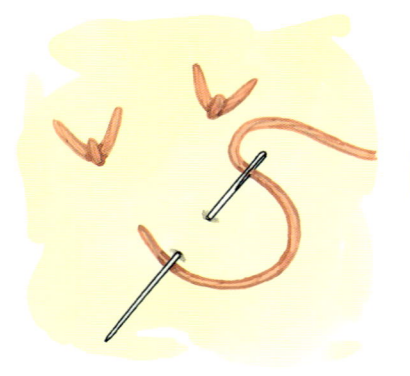

Fly stitch is a versatile stitch in which the shape can be varied and the fastening stitch can be long or short. It is worked in a similar way to lazy daisy (see opposite) except that the needle is inserted a small distance away from where it emerges from the fabric and is brought up again through the loop. Fasten the loop with a vertical stitch.

Slipstitch

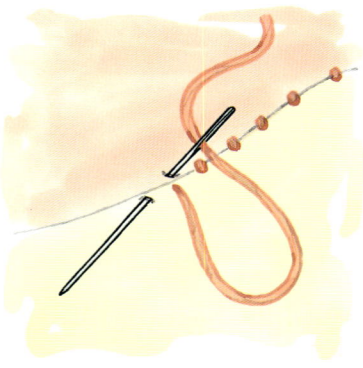

This is an unobtrusive stitch used mainly for attaching appliqué fabric, or for sewing on bindings and trimmings.

Bring the needle up through the background fabric close to the edge of the applique motif and take a tiny stitch into the turned edge. Work a second stitch approximately ¼ inch/ 5 mm from the first.

Seed stitch

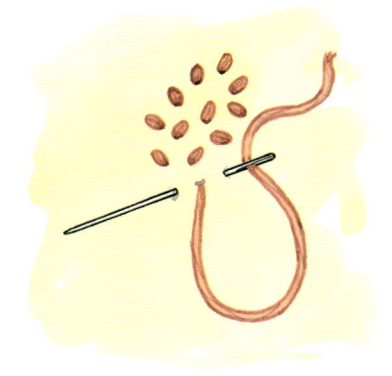

Seed stitch is used to fill a design area by creating numerous straight stitches of equal length placed randomly. Bring out the thread and take it down to make a short stitch, then bring it up again a short distance from the first stitch, in a slightly different direction.

STITCHES

Herringbone stitch

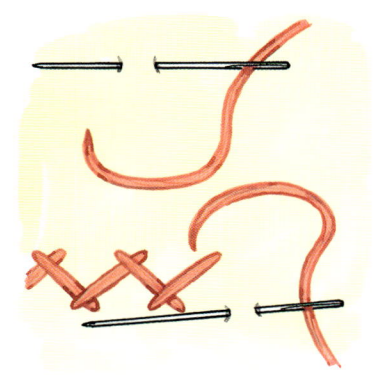

Herringbone is suitable for creating a decorative band or for securing appliqué. Working from left to right, bring the needle out on the lower stitching line and take a diagonal stitch to the upper stitching line. Bring the needle up a short distance to the left and take a diagonal stitch to the lower stitching line, crossing the first. Bring the needle up to the left as before and repeat. This stitch can also be used in counted-thread embroidery, usually over four intersections of fabric threads. A solid band of stitches is produced by working a second row directly below the first but overlapping it, and following the same procedure for subsequent rows.

Cross stitch

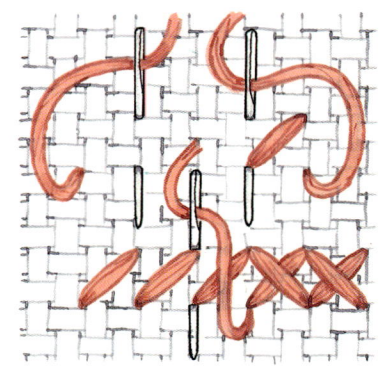

The cross stitch is made of two half cross stitches. Each half cross stitch is made diagonally over two threads of evenweave fabric, usually from bottom left to top right. To complete the cross stitch, work another stitch diagonally on top from bottom right to top left. It is essential to retain the same direction while working a particular area of the design. If working a line or block of cross stitch, work the entire area in half cross stitch before completing the second crossing stitches.

Satin stitch

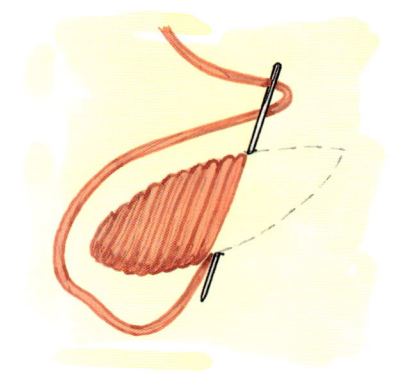

Satin stitch consists of a series of straight parallel stitches, lying close together. Wherever possible work them diagonally across a shape to preserve a well-defined outline. Limit the length of the stitches to ½ inch/ 12 mm, and allow the threads to lie smoothly on the surface without twisting.

Bring the needle up on one edge of the shape to be embroidered and insert it diagonally across on the opposite edge. Bring the needle up alongside the start of the first stitch and insert it again on the opposite edge to produce a long stitch parallel to the first. On evenweave fabric, the stitches can be more easily worked in a vertical or horizontal direction.

Lazy daisy stitch

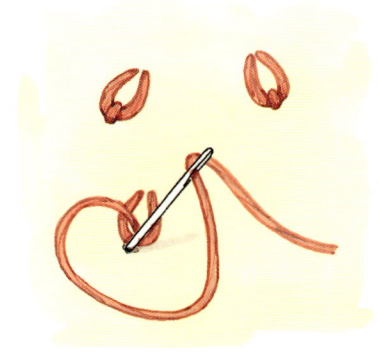

Lazy daisy, also known as detached chain stitch, is often used to create flower petals or small leaves, but it is also useful simply as a tiny motif, either in a formal pattern or scattered across an area.

Bring the needle out at the base of the petal shape and insert it again into the same hole, leaving a loop. Bring it up through the loop at the other end of the petal shape, pull the thread through (not too taut), and secure the loop with a small vertical stitch.

EMBELLISHED EMBROIDERY KIT

Buttonhole stitch

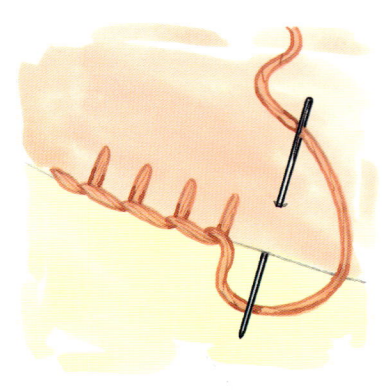

Also known as blanket stitch, buttonhole stitch is useful not only as a decorative stitch but also as an edging for appliqué. Working from left to right, bring the needle out on the bottom stitching line or the edge of the appliqué; insert it at the top stitching line and bring it out again, alongside the first stitch, taking it over the looped thread. Take it down again on the upper line and up through the loop as before. Repeat to create an edging of evenly spaced stitches. To finish, secure with a small stitch holding the last loop.

Couching

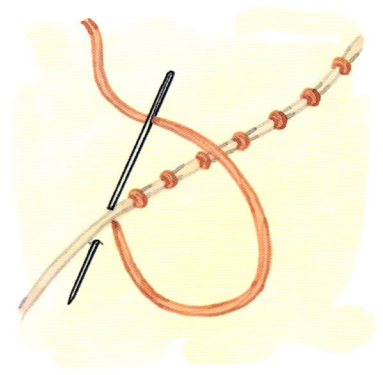

Threads are laid on the surface and secured by small stitches, at regular intervals,. Bring out the thread to be couched at the start of the stitching line. Bring a second thread up a short distance along the stitching line. Hold the couched thread taut and take a small vertical stitch over it with the second thread. Fasten off.at the back.

Feather stitch

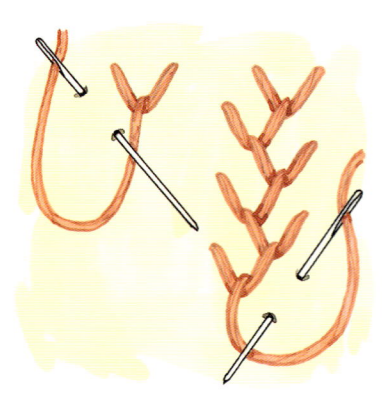

The feather stitch is really a series of continuous fly stitches. Bring the needle out at top left and insert it at top right, keeping the thread toward you to form a loop. Bring the needle up through the loop and repeat the whole stitch slightly below and to the left. Continue working from side to side.

Stem stitch

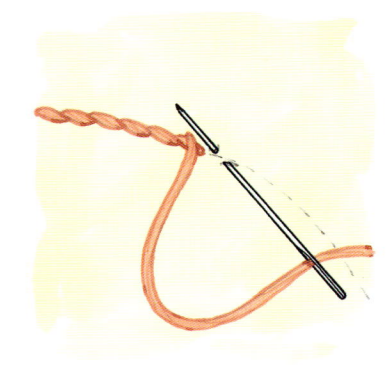

Stem stitch produces a rope-like line and, as the name implies, is often used for the stems of vegetation. It is also useful for outlining shapes and, if worked in closely packed formation, can act as a filling stitch.

Working from left to right, bring the needle out on the stitching line and take it down a short distance along again on the stitching line. Keeping the thread loosely above the stitching line, bring the needle up again halfway along the length of the first stitch. Pull the stitch tight and repeat.

French knots

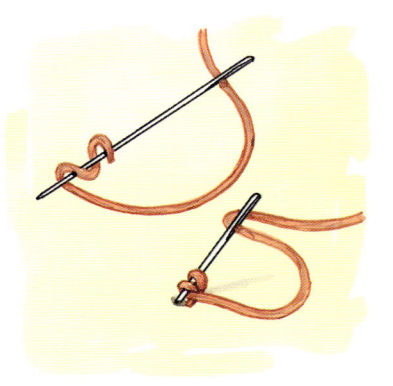

French knots are useful for the centers of flowers and for dotted lines. They can also be scattered randomly. Bring the needle up, hold the thread taut between the forefinger and thumb of your non-working hand, and twist the needle around the thread once or twice. Insert the needle partway into the fabric at a point just adjacent to where the thread emerged, pull the twist down the needle so that it lies on the fabric, then pull the needle through quickly and smoothly to the back of the work.

Left-handed readers

When working stitches in the hand, reverse the direction shown. When using a frame, you can stitch in any direction, as the needle is inserted vertically through the fabric.

The Kit Components

Your kit contains all you need, apart from a small piece of card, to make three of the projects in the book: Beaded Trinket Box, Elegant Evening Bag and Ribbon Embroidery Hair Slide. You will find templates for these projects on page 44.

ELEGANT EVENING BAG
(see page 18)

Navy satin 8
Blue cotton thread 4
Purple embroidery thread 11
Blue cord (For the strap) 10
Metal button 13
Purple lining fabric 2
Batting (wadding) 3
Rocaille beads 5
Bugle beads 7

RIBBON EMBROIDERY HAIR SLIDE
(see page 20)

Batting (wadding) 12
Embroidery thread In green and cream for stems and for holding the ribbon bows 14 & 15
Ribbon (4mm wide) In three shades of pink and peach, green and yellow for the ribbon flower embroidery decoration 17
Hair slide attachment 16
Cream satin fabric 1

BEADED TRINKET BOX
(see page 16)

Cream cotton thread 6
Round opalescent bead for central flower motif 9
Cream satin fabric 1
Purple lining fabric 2
Batting (wadding) 3
Rocaille beads 5
Bugle beads 7

15

EMBELLISHED EMBROIDERY KIT

Beaded Trinket Box

Boxes make delightful gifts, and this satin and beaded example, with its contrasting lining, is no exception. A little girl will find it just the thing to keep her treasures safe. Your best friend will be delighted to receive one to hold her rings, earrings, or other small, precious things.

MATERIALS PROVIDED:

- Cream satin
- Purple lining
- Rocaille beads
- Bugle beads
- Round bead
- Batting (wadding)
- Cream sewing thread

OTHER MATERIALS AND EQUIPMENT

- Fine white cotton backing fabric for satin, 8 x 8 inches/20 x 20 cm
- Cream-colored strong poster board (card) or mat (mounting) board 12 x 8 inches/30 x 20 cm
- Steel rule, craft knife, and cutting mat
- Fabric glue
- Hard pencil
- Fine needles or beading needles
- Basic sewing equipment
- 6-inch-/15-cm-diameter embroidery hoop
- Masking tape
- Template (see page 44)

1 From the cream satin, cut two squares, 4½ x 4½ inch/ 12 x 12 cm, for the top and the base, and four rectangles, 4½ x 2½ inch/12 x 7 cm, for the sides. From the purple fabric, cut two squares, 4½ x 4½ inch/ 12 x 12 cm, for the inner top and inner base and four rectangles, 4½ x 2½ inch/ 12 x 7 cm for the sides.

2 To transfer the flower design, first center it beneath one piece of cream satin; use masking tape to keep it in place, and trace through lightly with a hard pencil.

3 Baste (tack) the top fabric to the square of white cotton fabric around the edges, and mount the fabric in the embroidery hoop.

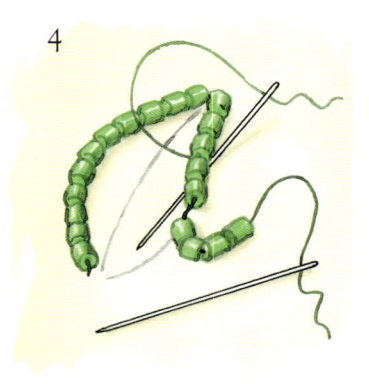

4

4 Sew the beads on using the couching method. Bring the needle up through the wrong side of the fabric and thread the required number of beads. Lay the beads along the line of the design. Using a second needle and thread, take a tiny stitch across the row of beads, between each bead or every two or three beads, depending on the intricacy of the design (see fig. 4). Outline the leaves with green rocaille beads in this way, and then work their central veins. Outline the flower petals in blue rocaille beads, and fill in the three main petals. Sew the large round bead in the center. For the stem, start alongside the flower, and couch green bugle and rocaille beads alternately. Add small scattered beads, singly and in groups of three and six, around the flower.

5 Using the steel rule and craft knife, cut the mat (mounting) board into the following pieces: 3½ x 3½ inches/9 x 9 cm for the top and base; four pieces 3½ x 1½ inches/9 x 4 cm for the sides; and two pieces 3¼ x 3¼ inches/8.5 x 8.5 cm for the inner base and inner top.

BEADED TRINKET BOX

6 Center the base board, cream side down, on the wrong side of the cream satin base. Spread a small amount of fabric glue around the edge of the wrong side of the board, and fold the fabric edges over, pulling it taut (see fig. 6). Complete the four sides and the inner top in the same way.

7 Cut a square of batting (wadding) to fit the top, and carefully pull it apart to halve the thickness. Cover the beaded top as for the base board, but place one half of the batting between the board and fabric. Use the other half of the batting for the inner base, covering this in the same way.

8 To line the sides, fold and press hems around all four edges of the lining to fit the sides, then slipstitch in place.

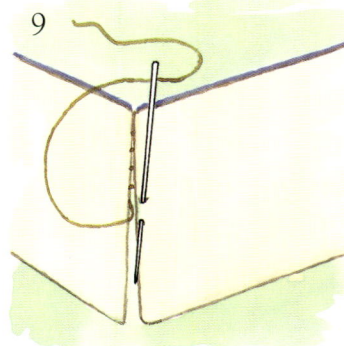

9 To assemble the box, first sew the four sides together using ladder stitch and working on the right side of the box. Holding two sides parallel, bring the needle out through the folded edge on one side and insert it directly opposite through the folded edge on the other side. Take the needle through the fold and out again a short way along, then take it across to the first side. After working several stitches, pull the thread tight, then continue as before (see fig. 9).

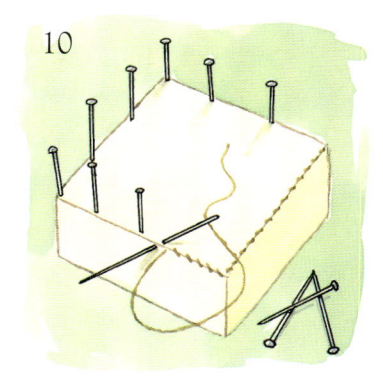

10 Place the base of the box on top of the four sides and insert pins to keep it rigid (see fig. 10). Overcast the sides to the base.

11 Stick the uncovered side of the inner base to the bottom of the box. Glue the inner lid to the lid.

Tips
• Mounting the satin on a larger piece of fine backing fabric supports the beadwork and makes it easier to mount in an embroidery hoop.

Variations
• Attach the lid to the box by sewing it along one side using ladder stitch.
• Use this box-making method to make other box shapes, such as rectangles, or triangles.
• Pad the outside or inside of the sides of larger boxes with thin batting (wadding).

17

EMBELLISHED EMBROIDERY KIT

Elegant Evening Bag

This evening bag can accompany you on all your late-night dates. It is just large enough to hold the bare necessities, and will add a touch of glamor to your favorite evening ensemble. The design is embroidered in satin stitch with fine lines in stem stitch, and trimmed with beads, a covered button, and cord.

MATERIALS PROVIDED

- Navy satin
- Purple lining
- Navy sewing thread
- Purple stranded embroidery floss
- 25 blue bugle beads
- 35 blue rocaille beads
- Button
- Batting (wadding)
- Cord

OTHER MATERIALS AND EQUIPMENT

- Fine white cotton backing fabric 14 x 8 inches/36 x 20 cm
- White dressmaker's carbon paper and ballpoint pen
- 6-inch-/15-cm-diameter embroidery hoop
- Fine crewel embroidery needle and beading needle
- Basic sewing equipment
- Tracing paper and pencil
- Template (see page 44)

1 Trace the design and transfer it to the satin using dressmaker's carbon (see page 11). Cut out the satin, with a ⅝-inch/1.5-cm seam allowance.

2 Baste (tack) the satin to the rectangle of white cotton fabric around the edges, and mount in the embroidery hoop.

3 Using two strands of floss, work the main areas of the design in satin stitch (see page 13) and the single lines in stem stitch (see page 14). (You will need to re-mount the fabric to complete the stitching.)

4 Trim off the excess backing fabric. Cut a piece of batting (wadding) to fit the embroidered satin, and carefully pull it apart to halve the thickness. Cut the lining fabric the same size.

ELEGANT EVENING BAG

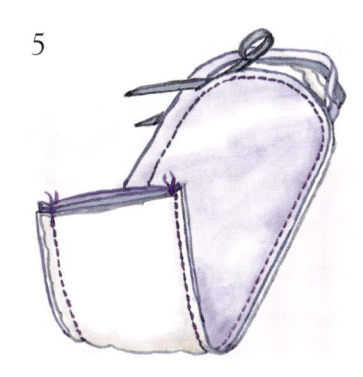

5 Place the satin right side up on the batting (wadding) and lay the lining on top. Pin and baste (tack) the three layers together, then stitch around the edges along the seam line, either by hand, using backstitch, or by machine, leaving the short side open (see fig. 5). Trim the excess batting to the seam and the fabrics to within ¼ inch/5 mm. Clip the curve.

6 Turn the bag right side out and lightly press the edges. Fold a hem along the top edge and slipstitch the lining to the satin.

7 Fold the front of the bag up on the fold line and overcast the sides together. Press the flap down on the other fold line.

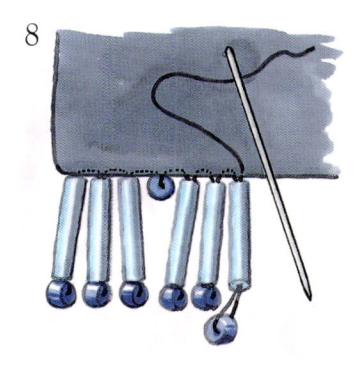

8 For the bead trim along the bottom edge, sew two bugle beads at each corner, then sew alternate groups of three blue bugle beads, each topped with a rocaille bead, and single rocaille beads. To sew the bugle/rocaille bead trim, bring the thread through both beads, then return it through the bugle bead (see fig. 8).

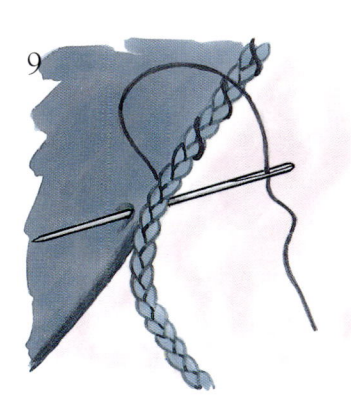

9 Adjust the cord size to fit the sides of the bag, with extra for the handle. Secure the ends by winding a thread around the cord ½ inch/1 cm from each end (see fig. 9). Stitch the cord to the sides of the bag with invisible stitches.

10 To make the covered button, cut a 1½-inch/4-cm-diameter circle from the lining fabric. At the center, sew a single blue rocaille bead and add four radiating lazy daisy stitches (see page 13) surrounding it. Work running stitches ¼ inch/5 mm from the edge. Pull up the gathers and insert the metal button. Trim the edges of the fabric neatly, and secure firmly. Stitch to the front of the bag.

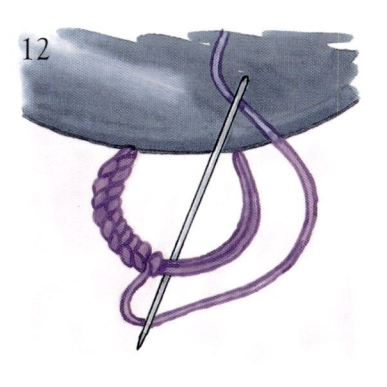

12 Work a button loop at the base of the bag flap. Using six strands of stranded floss, make two loose stitches big enough to accommodate the button. Starting at the left side of this loop, work buttonhole stitches until the loose stitches are covered (see fig. 12).

Tips
• For a smooth-edged motif, work satin stitch diagonally across the shape, with stitches that are not more than ½ inch/1 cm long.
• When working stem stitch, make the stitches smaller at sharp curves in the design.
• Before sewing the bead trim, strengthen your thread by drawing it through a block of beeswax. This will also prevent the thread from twisting.

Variations
• Use the design for other projects, either singly for small items or as a repeat motif on larger bags or cushions.
• Use the bag shape for projects incorporating other embroidery techniques, such as quilting, stitchery, or counted thread work on evenweave material.
• For a 1920s effect, create a fringe by lengthening the bead trim with extra bugle beads.

EMBELLISHED EMBROIDERY KIT

Ribbon Embroidery Hair Slide

Popular in Victorian times, ribbon embroidery is now enjoying a revival. Delicate silk ribbons are used to create three-dimensional effects, which can be extremely pretty, as this charming hair slide demonstrates. Just three stitches are used for the ribbon work: straight stitch, lazy daisy, and woven wheels.

MATERIALS PROVIDED

- Cream satin
- Felt backing
- Batting (wadding)
- Green ribbon
- Dark pink ribbon
- Pink ribbon
- Pale pink ribbon
- Peach ribbon
- Yellow ribbon
- Cream sewing thread
- Metal hair slide
- Stranded embroidery floss in cream and green

OTHER MATERIALS AND EQUIPMENT

- White cotton backing fabric 8 x 8 inches/20 x 20 cm
- Hard pencil
- 6-inch-/15-cm-diameter embroidery hoop
- Tracing paper
- Large chenille needle
- Crewel embroidery needle
- Fabric glue
- Cardboard 4 x 3 inches/10 x 8 cm
- Masking tape
- Basic sewing equipment
- Template (see page 44)

1 Trace the template provided. Using masking tape, fix the tracing to a firm surface. Center the cream satin over it, and trace the design with the hard pencil, including the cutting line but not the inner fold line.

2 Place the satin over the cotton backing fabric, and baste (tack) them together around the edges. Mount the fabrics in the embroidery hoop.

3 Using the green ribbon in the chenille needle, work six straight stitches in the positions shown to represent stems, overlapping the stitches at the top. Work five lazy daisy stitches (see page 13) for leaves.

4 Using two strands of green embroidery floss in the crewel needle, work additional stems in stem stitch (see page 14), and add small leaves in lazy daisy stitch (see page 13). Work a fly stitch (see page 12) at the top of each stem for the seven rosebuds.

5 Using peach ribbon in the chenille needle, work two flowers in lazy daisy stitch, with four petals each. Work two more flowers in the same way, using yellow ribbon.

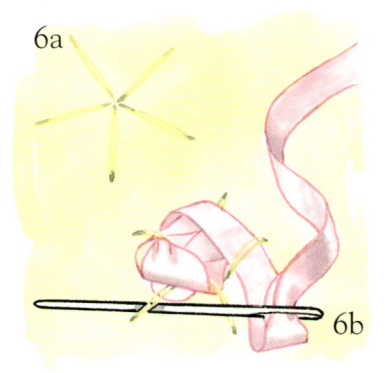

6a

6b

6 Using pink and dark pink ribbon, work woven wheels for the six roses. First lay the foundation for each rose, using two strands of cream floss in the crewel needle. Work five short, radiating stitches into a central point (see fig. 6a). Then, starting at the center, weave the ribbon over and under these stitches alternately until the spokes of the wheel are covered (see fig. 6b). Take the needle through to the back of the work and fasten off.

RIBBON EMBROIDERY HAIR SLIDE

7 For the rosebuds, use pink and dark pink ribbon and lazy daisy and single straight stitches, to vary the size.

8 Cut the pale pink ribbon in half. Tie each piece in a neat bow, and sew them in place, one on top of the other, as shown in the photograph, using cream sewing thread and concealing the stitches under the knot. Hold the loops and ends of the bows with tiny, invisible stitches, using a single strand of cream floss.

9 Remove the work from the hoop. Trim away the excess fabric (both layers) along the cutting line. Trim the traced paper design along the fold line, and use this as a template to trace and cut an oval shape from the cardboard. Use the cardboard shape as a template to cut an oval from batting (wadding) and one from felt. Gently pull the batting apart to halve its thickness.

10 Place the embroidery face down on a soft surface, and place the cardboard on top. Draw around the edge, trim the backing fabric along this line, and clip the edges of the satin to within ¼ inch/5 mm of the edge of the backing (see fig. 10).

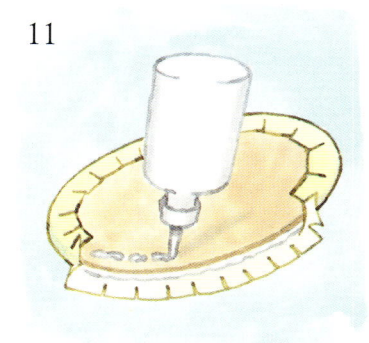

11 Apply a small dot of glue to the center of the cardboard oval and stick the batting (wadding) to it. Place the cardboard, batting side down, on the wrong side of the embroidery. Apply glue around the cardboard edge. Fold the fabric over the cardboard to stick in place, pulling them taut (see fig. 11).

12 Trim the edges of the felt oval slightly to make it smaller than the fabric-covered card. Glue or stitch it in place. Firmly stitch the metal hair slide to the wrong side.

Tips
• When starting and finishing stitching with ribbon, leave a short length free. Using sewing thread, stitch this firmly to the backing fabric, then trim off the excess ribbon.
• Always cut ribbons on the diagonal to prevent fraying.
• When stitching, do not pull the ribbon too tight, but allow it to lie softly on the surface.

Variations
• You could adapt this design to decorate childrens' or babies' clothes.
• Make two identical ribbon-embroidered ovals entirely in one color, such as black or navy, and attach them to clips for adding to a pair of plain evening shoes.
• Try out other conventional embroidery stitches, using ribbons of different widths. If experimenting with wider ribbons, use a loosely woven fabric.

21

EMBELLISHED EMBROIDERY KIT

Appliqué Folk Art Picture

The naive quality of this attractive appliqué picture is reminiscent of the work of pioneer women, who would use scraps of fabric from worn garments not only for pictorial motifs on quilts but also in pictures for the walls of their homes.

MATERIALS AND EQUIPMENT

- Unbleached muslin (calico) 9 x 12 inches/23 x 30 cm
- Cotton fabric for lining the picture 13 x 17 inches/ 33 x 43 cm
- Scraps of cotton fabric in small-print designs, plaids, and solid colors
- Matching sewing thread
- Thread for basting (tacking)
- 6 buttons
- 6 small beads
- Tracing paper and pencil
- Standard embroidery floss in brown, green, and rust
- Basic sewing equipment
- Template (see page 45)

1 Trace the picture motifs, and cut them out from the cotton scraps, including a ¼-inch/5-mm seam allowance.

2 Pin the templates to the wrong side of the fabric pieces. Clip the curves to within ⅛ inch/3 mm of the template, clip into inner corners, and trim off excess fabric at the points. Fold and baste (tack) the fabric edges over the paper, gathering as necessary (see fig. 2). Press and remove all basting (tacking) stitches.

3 Cut 6 bias strips from the green fabric, each ¾ inch/ 2 cm wide, for the stems. Press under ¼ inch/5 mm along each long edge (see fig. 3.)

Tips
- Wash and iron all new fabrics before use.
- To achieve the muted effect of an old-style folk picture, immerse the fabrics in tea or coffee for a few minutes, then rinse, dry, and iron before use.

4 Using the pattern as a guide, assemble the pieces in the center of the muslin (calico). Baste (tack) the lower flowerpot piece and the stems first, then add the flowers, leaves, and bud, covering the raw edges of the stems with the top of the flowerpot. Baste (tack) the bird in position and add the wing. Slipstitch all the pieces in place (see fig. 4). Remove the basting (tacking) and press lightly.

APPLIQUE FOLK ART PICTURE

5 Using two strands of embroidery floss, work the veins of the leaves with fly stitch (see page 12); work five rows of fly stitch for the bird's tail. Add legs, feet, and crest in straight stitches. Sew on a small bead for the eye and five beads on the crest (see fig. 5). Work herringbone stitch along the length of some of the stems and French knots radiating from the top of the hearts.

6 For the frame, cut several strips of fabric from the cotton scraps about 1½ inches/ 4 cm wide. Press under a turning along the long edge of each piece. Following the picture, arrange two rows around the picture in random fashion. Pin and slipstitch in place. Press a ½-inch/1-cm turning to the back. Pin a row of strips around the edge of the muslin (calico), overlapping its raw edge with the turned edges of strips and similarly lapping one strip end over its neighbor. Add short strips, if necessary, at the corners. Slipstitch the strips in place. Add another row in the same way to the first row. Press under ½ inch/1 cm on the raw edges all around (see fig. 6).

7 Sew buttons at the center of the flowers and surround with a series of detached chain stitches. Add more buttons at the corners of the frame.

8 Fold under the edges of the lining fabric to fit the picture. Slipstitch in place.

Variations
• Similar motifs look good on cushions, or quilts.
• For a more contemporary effect, choose bright primary colors on a white background.

EMBELLISHED EMBROIDERY KIT

Jeweled Picture Frame

Bring a touch of glamor into your living room or bedroom with this extravagantly decorated picture frame. A favorite photograph or a mirror can be given a theatrical treatment with a frame of ruched fabric and fake jewels.

MATERIALS AND EQUIPMENT

- 2 pieces cream satin fabric each 8 x 7 inches/20 x 18 cm
- Sheer yellow-gold fabric 10 x 11 inches/25 x 28 cm
- Fine cotton fabric for backing 12 x 12 inches/30 x 30 cm
- 14 flat-backed fake jewels in different shapes and sizes
- Bronze sequins
- Blue sequins
- Yellow sewing thread
- Gold cord 8 inches/20 cm long
- 2-piece picture mat (mount), 6¾ x 5 inches/17 x 13 cm, with oval opening
- Thin batting (wadding) 6¾ x 5 inches/17 x 13 cm
- Gold poster board (card) 5 x 4 inches/13 x 10 cm
- Beading needle
- Crewel embroidery needle
- 10-inch-/25-cm-diameter embroidery hoop
- Spray adhesive and fabric glue
- Fabric marker or hard pencil
- Basic sewing equipment

1 Center the window mat (mount) on one piece of satin and, using marker or pencil, lightly mark around the inner and outer edges.

2 Mount the backing fabric in the hoop. Baste (tack) the satin to the backing, centering it and aligning the fabric grains. Lay the sheer fabric on top, again with fabric grains aligned.

3 Arrange the jewels randomly on the mat (mount) in a pleasing design; use this as your stitching guide.

Tips
- For a hanging frame, sew a piece of cord to the back.
- For a standing frame, cover a strip of cardboard with fabric, and sew it to the back, 2 inches/5 cm from the top.
- To prevent cord from unraveling, cover each end with a small piece of transparent tape.

JEWELED PICTURE FRAME

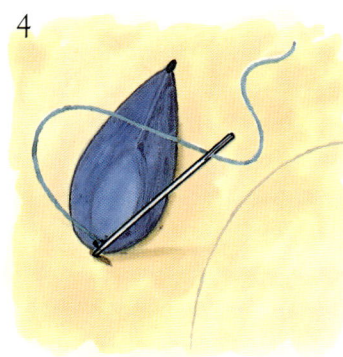

4 Sew the jewels so that the fabric gathers between them. Start at the opening, and work outward. Sew in place using a beading needle (see fig. 4).

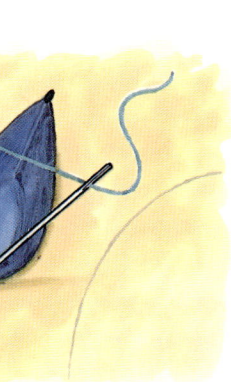

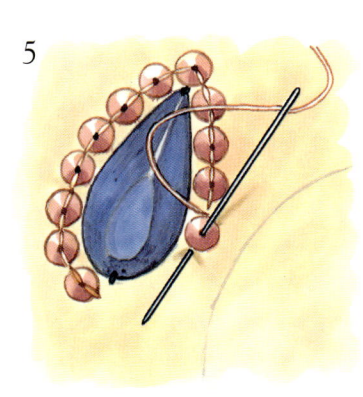

5 To surround the jewel with sequins, sew on each sequin with two backstitches, parallel to the edge of the jewel (see fig. 5).

6 Gather the fabric in ruches around the jewel and secure them with a few small stitches in the folds.

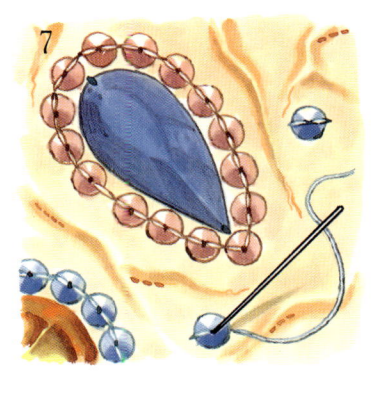

7 Continue adding the jewels and gathering the fabric. Add sequins randomly (see fig. 7). Remove from the hoop, and cut off excess backing fabric.

8 Spray adhesive on the front of the mount and lay the batting (wadding) on top. Trim.

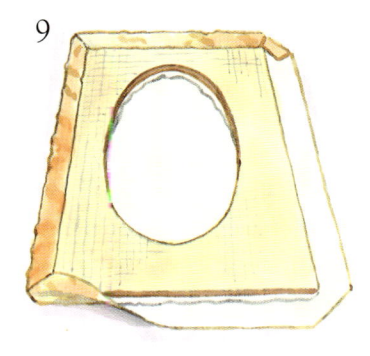

9 Place the embroidered fabric face down, then position the mat (mount) on top, with the batting underneath. Trim the fabric to measure 1 inch/2.5 cm larger all around than the frame. Fold the edges over the back of the mat (mount) and glue down. Trim excess fabric at corner folds (see fig. 9).

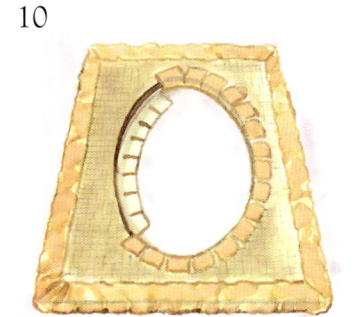

10 Cut out the center oval. Clip the fabric to ½ inch/5 mm of the mat (mount) edge. Fold to the wrong side, and glue in place (see fig. 10).

11 Starting at the center top, sew the gold cord around the opening. Tuck the ends to the back and sew in place.

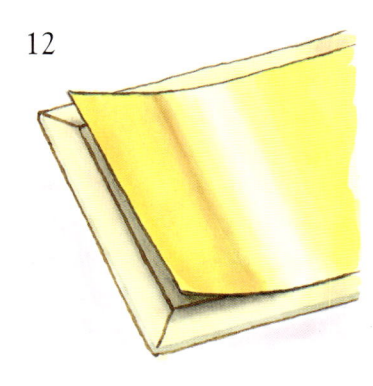

12 For the frame back, cover the other mat (mount) part with the other piece of satin, cut 1 inch/2.5 cm larger all around than the frame. Fold the edges over the back and glue in place. Cut off excess fabric at corner folds. Center the gold poster board (card) on the uncovered side and glue in place (see fig. 12).

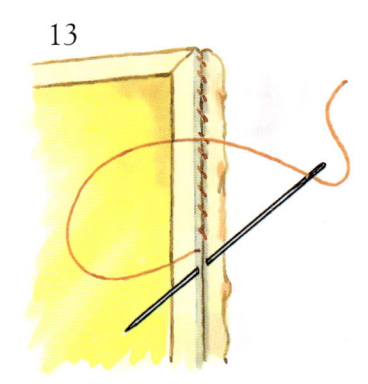

13 Place the frame front and back together with wrong sides facing. Overcast the edges together on three sides (see fig. 13), leaving the fourth open; insert a picture.

Variations
• Try other shapes and sizes of frames; ovals and circles are good for portraits, horizontals for town scenes and landscapes.
• Make a frame for wedding photos using leftovers from the bride's or bridesmaids' dresses.
• As an alternative to fake jewels, use large sequin shapes, such as flowers, hearts, or diamonds.
• Cover a bathroom mirror frame in crisp cotton fabric and decorate it with shells. Sew on shells that have holes.

EMBELLISHED EMBROIDERY KIT

Victorian Valentine Pincushion

During the nineteenth century, people often made romantic souvenir pincushions as gifts for their loved ones on occasions such as christenings, weddings, and birthdays. Not only women made pincushions; soldiers and sailors made them for their sweethearts, decorating them with regimental badges and maritime motifs.

MATERIALS AND EQUIPMENT

- Orange velvet
  8 x 8 inches/20 x 20 cm
- Thick silver thread for couching
- Gray sewing thread
- 2 pieces lilac silk
  6 x 8 inches/15 x 20 cm
- Bonding web (Bondaweb)
  4 x 4 inches/10 x 10 cm
- Bag of sawdust and funnel
- 60 inches/1.5 m of
  1¼-inch-/3-cm-wide mauve lace
- Heart-, star-, and flower-shaped sequins
- Spray of silk lilac flowers
- Small gold beads
- Purple beads
- Tracing paper and pencil
- Fabric marking pen
- 6-inch/15-cm diameter embroidery hoop
- Fine needle or beading equipment
- Basic sewing equipment
- Template (see page 45)

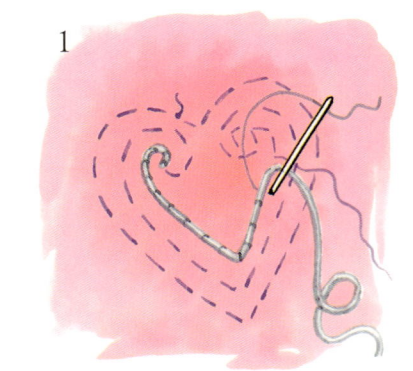

1 Trace the template and transfer the lines onto the velvet, using the trace and baste (tacking) method (see page 11). Mount the fabric in the hoop. Couch (see page 14) the silver thread along the inner lines, removing the basting stitches as you go (see fig. 1).

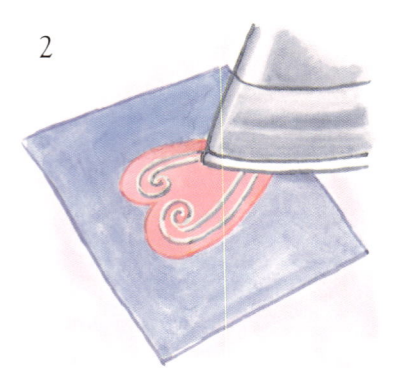

2 Center the bonding web over the stitching on the wrong side of the velvet, and press with a cool iron. From the right side, cut out the heart, leaving a ¼-inch/5-mm margin around it. Peel off the backing paper. Center the heart on one of the lilac silk rectangles and iron in place (see fig. 2).

3 With right sides facing, stitch the two rectangles together, either by machine or by hand, using backstitch, taking a ½-inch/1-cm seam allowance and leaving a 2-inch/5-cm opening on one side. Trim the excess fabric from the corners, and turn right side out through the opening. Use a funnel to fill the pincushion with sawdust, packing it down until it is tightly stuffed. Slipstitch the opening edges firmly together.

VICTORIAN VALENTINE PINCUSHION

4 Join the two ends of the lace with a narrow French seam (closing both raw edges). Fold the lace in half and in half again, and mark the folds at the straight edge. Gather the straight edge, and draw it up to fit the pincushion. Matching the fold marks to the corners of the pincushion, pin the lace in place, allowing extra fullness at the corners (see fig. 4). Adjust the gathers to lie evenly and slipstitch in place.

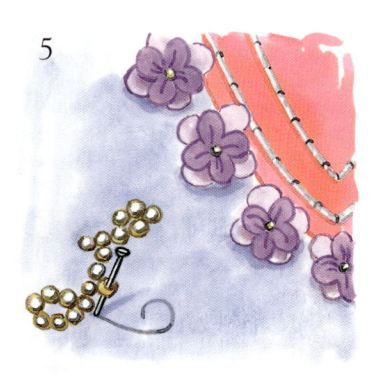

5 Snip off single flowers from the lilac spray and pin them around the heart, covering the raw edges and pushing the pins straight down into the filling.

With the fabric marking pen, write two initials on either side of the heart; pin a series of gold beads along the line (see fig. 5). Pin the other beads and sequins around the central motif.

Tips
- Use brass pins or other rust-resistant pins that will not mark the fabric.
- Dye white lace with small amounts of cold-water dye.

Variations
- Make a selection of pincushions in different shapes; squares, circles, ovals, hearts, and triangles are all suitable.
- The main fabric can be velvet, wool, or cotton, and the lace trim can be replaced with a braid, cord, or crochet edging.
- Alternative decorations include ribbon roses and a selection of lace motifs.
- A good alternative filling is bran. This traditional filling, which does not spoil, makes a good substitute for sawdust. Synthetic stuffing and absorbent cotton (cotton wool) are not recommended, as they are too lightweight and fluffy.

EMBELLISHED EMBROIDERY KIT

Sparkly Evening Purse

Whether you are going to the opera, to a Christmas party, or simply out to dinner, this tiny evening purse is just the thing to hold your lipstick and some small change. The sequins and beads add a touch of glamor to the fine fabric.

MATERIALS AND EQUIPMENT

- Red/blue woven silk shantung or dupion 15 x 8 inches/38 x 20 cm
- Purple silk lining fabric 15 x 8 inches/38 x 20 cm
- Small squares of synthetic silver metallic fabric and red silk, each about ½ x ½ inch/1 x 1 cm
- Stranded embroidery floss in fuchsia pink, navy blue, lavender, red, pink, pale pink, and very pale pink
- Assorted sequins and small glass beads (approximately 100)
- 3½ inches/9 cm of ⅛-inch-/3-mm-wide ribbon in gold, red, and purple, cut into ½-inch/1-cm pieces
- White fine nylon net 10½ x 5 inches/27 x 13 cm
- Worsted-weight cotton (double knit) fabric yarn: 28 inches/71 cm gold, 28 inches/71 cm purple, and 56 inches/142 cm red
- Rectangular embroidery frame large enough to hold the rectangle of silk fabric
- Beading needle
- Dressmaker's pins
- Crewel embroidery needle
- Fabric marker
- Basic sewing equipment

1 From both the silk shantung and the lining cut a rectangle 10½ x 7½ inches/ 27 x 18 cm. From the remaining pieces cut circles 3¾ inches/ 9.5 cm in diameter.

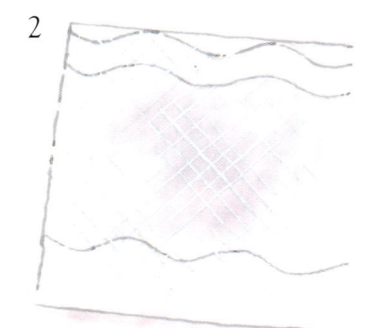

2 Cut a wavy line through the net, starting and finishing approximately 1 inch/3 cm from one long edge, to give one wide and one narrow strip. Trim the straight edges of these two strips in corresponding wavy lines (see fig. 2).

3 Arrange the cut squares of fabric, some of the pieces of ribbon, and the larger sequins randomly on the rectangle of main fabric. Sew them in place with the fabric yarn using running stitch, satin stitch, or buttonhole stitch for the fabric and ribbon and straight stitches to hold the sequins (see fig. 3).

4 Lay the strips of net on top, leaving a space between the two; pin and baste (tack) in place. Add more sequins, beads, and ribbon (reserving some for the tassels) on top of the net. Using sometimes one, sometimes two, strands of embroidery floss, embroider a sprinkling of seed stitches (see page 12) between the applied

5 Work rows of satin stitch to conceal and hold the edges of the net.

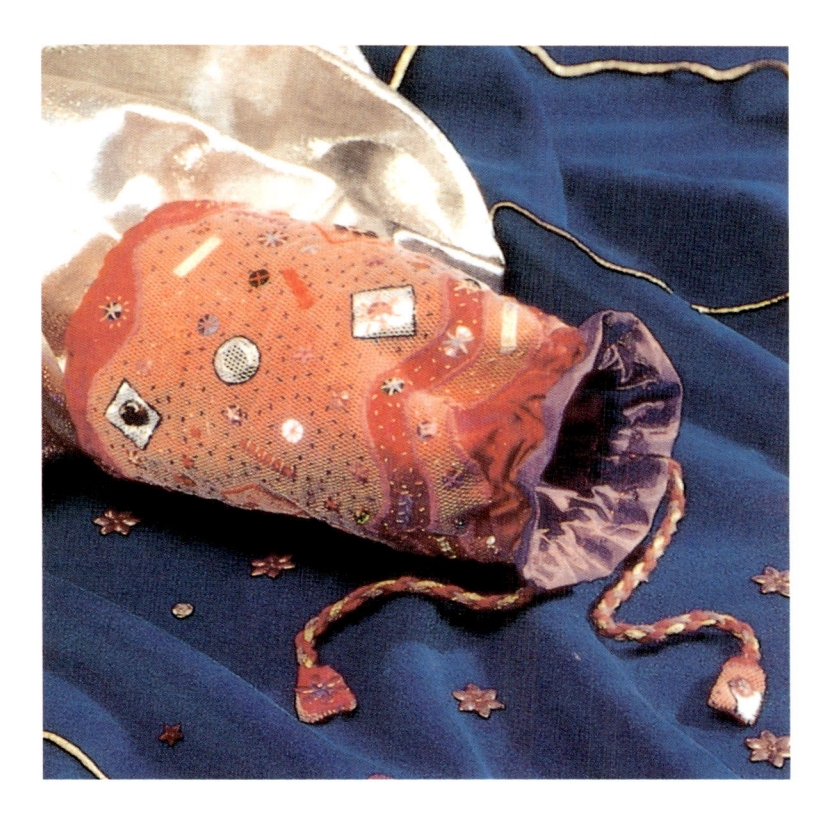

SPARKLY EVENING PURSE

Variations
- To make a larger purse, multiply all the measurements by 1.5.
- Try different fabrics, such as velvet, synthetic metallic fabric, brocade, or fine wool.

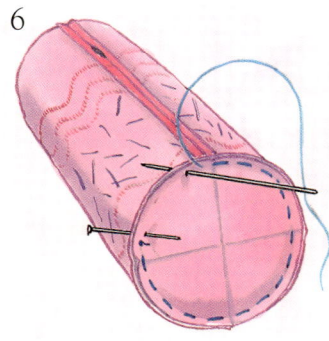

6 To assemble the purse, first fold the embroidered fabric in half with right sides together and short edges matching. Sew a firm seam in backstitch ¼ inch/5 mm from the raw edges to form a tube. Leave a small gap in the side seam for the drawstring, ¾ inch/2 cm from the top end. Fold the bottom circle in half and then in half again, and mark the folds at the edge. Fold the tube in half lengthwise and in half again, and mark the lower edge accordingly. Matching these marks, pin the bottom circle in place, using plenty of pins and easing the curves for a small effect. Baste (tack) and sew, using backstitch, ¼ inch/5 mm from the raw edges (see fig. 6).

7 Make the lining in a similar way, omitting the gap in the side seam.

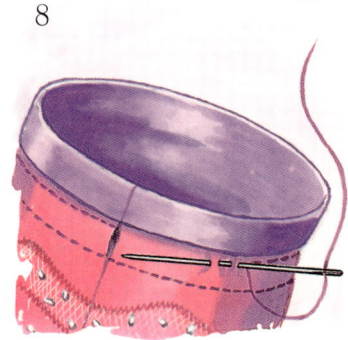

8 Insert the lining in the purse with wrong sides facing, and baste (tack) together close to the top edge. To form the ¼-inch/5-mm contrasting hem, fold the top edge over twice to the outside and slipstitch in place. To form the casing for the drawstring, work two parallel rows of running stitch below the hem, ½ inch/1 cm apart (see fig. 8).

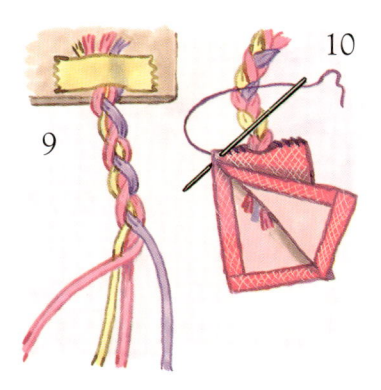

9 To make the braided cord for the drawstring, first cut the red yarn in half. Knot these two lengths together with the lengths of purple and gold yarn, and tape to the edge of a work table. Take one pair of yarns in each hand. Take the outside left yarn under the two center yarns and over the inside right, then return it to your left hand; take the outside right yarn under the two center yarns, over the inside left yarn and return it to your right hand (see fig. 9). When complete, knot the end. Attach a safety pin to one end and thread through the casing.

10 Cover the knots at the ends of the cord with small squares of fabric and net, whose edges have been turned under. Wrap these around the knots and slipstitch (see fig. 10) in place. Decorate with a few sequins and scraps of ribbon.

Tips
- Take care with silk fabrics, as they fray easily. Finish the edges of the seams with overcasting.

Wildflower Party Bolero

This charming bolero will complement a toddler's first party outfit and delight both mother and daughter. Daisies, forget-me-nots, and sprigs of clover, worked in simple stitches and enhanced with beads, are scattered in a delicate pattern. Made from a small piece of velvet, this bolero can be completed in just one evening.

MATERIALS AND EQUIPMENT

- Dark green velveteen (cotton velvet) 12 inches/30 cm long and 35 inches/90 cm wide
- Green satin 12 inches/30 cm long and 35 inches/90 cm wide
- Dark green sewing thread
- Stranded embroidery floss in green
- Lustrous rayon embroidery thread in pink and white
- Tiny glass beads in white, blue, and green
- Glass button
- Tracing paper
- Dressmaker's carbon paper in white
- Embroidery needle
- Beading needle
- Stretcher frame or 10-inch/25-cm embroidery hoop
- Basic sewing equipment
- Sewing machine
- Template (see page 45)

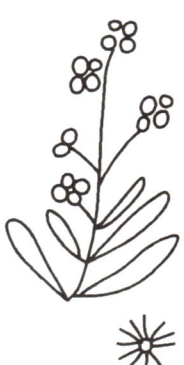

WILDFLOWER PARTY BOLERO

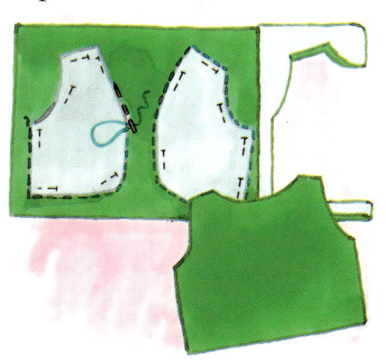

1 Trace the back and two fronts of the bolero pattern onto tracing paper and cut out. From the width of velvet, cut out the back on the fold. On the remaining fabric, place and pin the pattern pieces of the two fronts, leaving as much space as possible between them. Make sure the nap runs in the same direction on all pieces: downward for a lighter effect, upward for a darker one. Baste (tack) a marking line around the perimeter of each piece (see fig. 1). Using dressmaker's carbon paper (see page 11), transfer the flower and clover designs on both fronts.

2 Ideally, mount the fabric in a suitably sized stretcher frame (see page 6). If you are using an embroidery hoop, bind the rings with bias binding to avoid making a mark on the velvet.

3 With one strand of green embroidery floss, work the stems in stem stitch (see page 14) and the leaves in satin stitch (see page 13).

4 Work bullion knots as follows for the petals of the daisies and clover. First, slightly loosen the tension of the fabric in the frame. Bring the needle out at the center of the flowerhead and insert it at the end of the petal; then bring it halfway out at the starting point. Twist the thread around the needle, as many times as required to equal the length of the stitch (see fig. 4). Hold the twist with your thumb and pull the needle and thread smoothly through the fabric and the twist. Pull the needle and thread back toward the end of the petal and insert the needle there (see fig. 4a).

5 Using the beading needle, sew a white bead to the center of each daisy; use green beads for the clover leaves and blue beads for the forget-me-not flowers.

6 When the embroidery is complete, remove the work from the frame and cut out the two fronts on the basted (tacked) line. Cut out the satin lining back and two fronts.

7 To assemble the bolero, first place one front section and the back section together at their side edges with right sides facing. Pin and baste (tack) together, making a ⅝-inch/1.5-cm seam allowance. Repeat to join the other front section. Press the seams open. Join the lining in the same way. On the lining, press the shoulder seam allowances downward, with wrong sides facing.

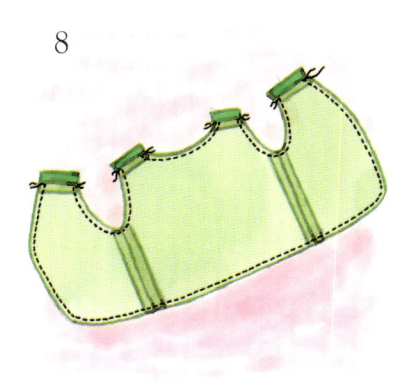

8 With right sides facing, pin the bolero and the lining together. Machine-stitch around the perimeter, omitting the shoulder seams (see fig. 8). Clip the curves and trim excess fabric. Turn right side out through one of the shoulder seam openings. Press lightly from the lining side.

9 To join the shoulder seams, pin the back and front raw edges of the velvet together and machine-stitch the seam, making sure not to catch in the lining. Slipstitch (see page 12) the folded edges of the back and front lining together.

10 On the right front, 5 inches/13 cm from the bottom edge, sew on a glass button. Work a button loop (see page 19) to match on the left front.

Tips
- If necessary, the twist in bullion knots can be adjusted by inserting the needle between the stitch and the fabric to ease the thread into place.
- If possible, place pins only within the seam allowance.
- To prevent the velvet and satin from sliding as you stitch, place tissue paper between them; pin, baste (tack), and stitch through all layers, then tear away the tissue paper.

Variations
- Use the pattern to make boleros in everyday fabrics such as denim, unbleached muslin (calico), and printed cotton.
- Use the embroidery motifs to decorate other pretty items for your children, for friends, or for yourself.

EMBELLISHED EMBROIDERY KIT

Wedding Ring Pillow

This special gift for a bride and groom will be a lasting memento of their wedding day. You can personalize it with the appropriate date and initials and add your own signature on the reverse side. Beads, sewn-on motifs, and a lace flounce give extra richness to the pillow.

MATERIALS AND EQUIPMENT

- 27-count cream linen 11 x 14 inches/28 x 36 cm
- Cream satin 11 x 14 inches/28 x 36 cm
- 5-inch-/13-cm-wide ready-gathered, double-edged lace flounce 52 inches/130 cm long
- Stranded embroidery floss in pale green, pale blue, and cream
- Fine synthetic gold metallic thread
- Cream pearl cotton No. 8
- Tiny rocaille beads in pale green, blue, pale blue, dark blue, pink, dark pink, white pearl
- 1 pink heart motif, 2 pink roses, 3 green leaves, and 8 flower-shaped beads
- Size 24 tapestry needle and beading needle
- Cream sewing thread
- 10-inch-/25-cm-diameter stretcher frame or embroidery hoop
- 13 x 10-inch/33 x 25-cm pillow form (cushion pad)
- Basic sewing equipment
- Template (see page 46)

1 Fold the linen in half from top to bottom and run a line of basting (tacking) stitches along the fold to mark the center line. Press the fabric and mount in a frame.

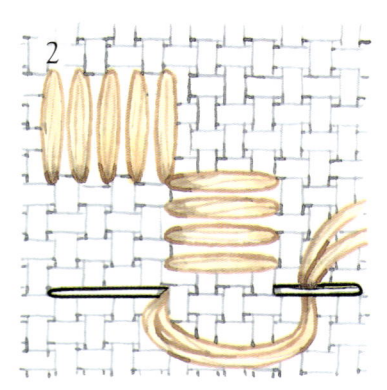

2 Referring to the chart on page 47, stitch Kloster blocks in cream pearl cotton, starting on the center line 4½ inches/11.5 cm from the top edge. Kloster blocks are worked in groups of five parallel satin stitches over four threads of fabric. U represents blocks of vertical stitches, and = represents horizontal blocks. Note that the end stitches of each block share a hole with the end stitches of adjacent blocks (see fig. 2).

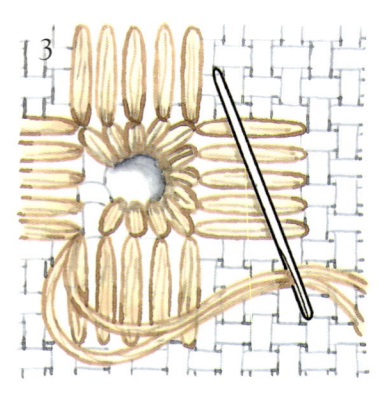

3 Work an eyelet in the center of each Kloster block. Start in one corner and go down in the center. Stitch clockwise, inserting the needle in the same central hole (see fig. 3).

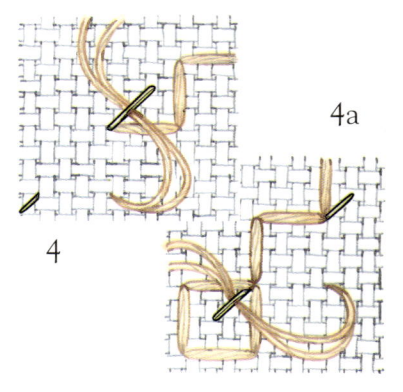

4 Fill the right hand heart with faggot stitch, using two strands of cream floss. Bring the needle out at the top of the diagonal line, insert it four threads to the right. Then bring it out four threads below the starting point, take it down into the starting point, and bring it out four threads down and four to the left. Repeat (see fig. 4). Work in the opposite direction to form squares (see fig. 4a).

WEDDING RING PILLOW

9 For the flower loops at the center top, come up at the center of the motif, thread ten pearl beads, and insert the needle in the same hole. Work five loops for each of the three flowers.

10 Finish by adding the pink heart, the two pink roses, the three green leaves, and the flower-shaped beads at the corners of the initial squares. Secure each with a pearl bead.

11 Placing the right sides together, stitch the embroidered linen and the satin backing together either by machine or using backstitch (see page 12). Take a ½-inch/ 1-cm seam allowance, leaving a 4-inch/10-cm opening on one side, through which to turn the work. Trim the excess fabric from the corners and turn right side out. Insert the pillow form (cushion pad) and slipstitch the opening edges together.

12 Pin the lace flounce around the seam, adding fullness at the corners, and hand-sew the two ends together. Sew the flounce in place with invisible stitches along the seam line and 1 inch/2.5 cm above it.

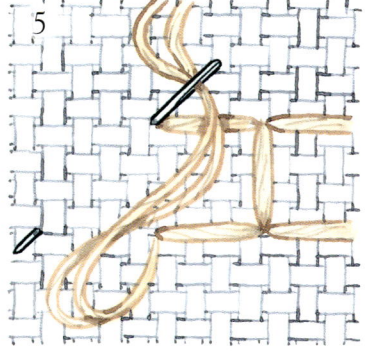

5 Fill the center of the left heart with four-sided stitch worked in horizontal and vertical rows, using two strands of floss. Each stitch consists of three backstitches, each over four threads, worked on three sides of a square and pulled tightly (see fig. 5). Finish the last square with a fourth stitch. A cross is formed on the back as the stitch is worked.

6 Work the border and leaves at the center top in two strands of pale green embroidery floss, in cross stitch (see page 13). Stitch the birds' bodies in pale blue cross stitch (two strands of floss) and the bows in a single strand of synthetic gold metallic thread.

7 Work the squares for the initials in four-sided stitch, using stranded cream embroidery floss as before.

8 Sew on the beads using cream floss and half cross stitch (see page 13). For the roses, use pink and dark pink beads; small flowers, pale and dark blue; the birds' wings, pale blue; the birds' eyes, blue; the border, pale green; the hearts and initials, white pearl.

EMBELLISHED EMBROIDERY KIT

Art Deco Brooch

The Art Deco style of the 1930s is one that never goes out of fashion, particularly for jewelry. This black and purple brooch captures the essence of that period, with the added texture and color of ribbon embroidery. Easy to make with beads and ribbon, it will enliven a plain sweater or sit well on a jacket lapel.

MATERIALS AND EQUIPMENT

- **Black perforated paper 5 x 5 inches/13 x 13 cm**
- **Stranded embroidery floss in black and lavender**
- **⅛-inch-/4-mm-wide ribbon in green, purple, and ombre (blended) rose/purple**
- **10 ¼-inch/5-mm bugle beads in iridescent black**
- **8 ⁵⁄₁₆-inch/9-mm bugle beads in iridescent black**
- **Rocaille beads in dark purple, plum, and iridescent black**
- **2 flower-shaped beads**
- **Tapestry needle, embroidery needle, and beading needle**
- **Brooch pin**
- **Basic sewing equipment**

1 Mark a central vertical line on the perforated paper with basting (tacking) stitches. (The smooth side of the paper is the right side.) Following the chart, work half cross stitches (see page 13) in four strands of black floss for the background.

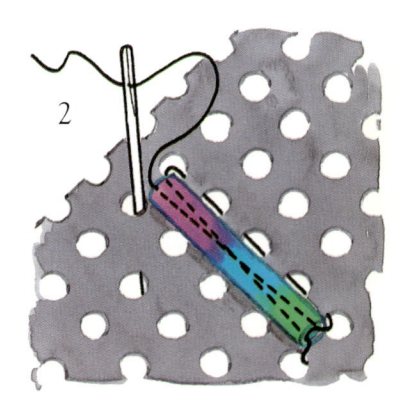

2 Using one strand of floss, add the large bugle beads with two stitches worked parallel in adjacent holes (see fig. 2). Add the small bugle beads diagonally and the black and purple rocaille beads with half cross stitches.

34

3 Work a woven wheel rose (see page 20) in purple ribbon on a base of two strands of lavender floss. In green ribbon, work lazy daisy stitches (see page 13) for the leaves. Fill in with French knots (see page 14) in blended rose/purple ribbon.

4 Work bead loop flowers each with five plum beads, and add the flower-shaped beads, securing each with a small black bead. To make the bead loop flowers, take the thread through the fabric then thread the plum beads onto the needle and thread. Insert the needle back into the same hole or an adjacent hole of fabric, so that the beads form a loop.

5 Sew or glue the brooch pin to the center back. With small sharp scissors, cut out the brooch one hole outside the stitched area.

Tips
- When sewing beads, strengthen the thread by drawing it through a block of beeswax.
- Make sure that all the rocaille beads lie in the same direction.

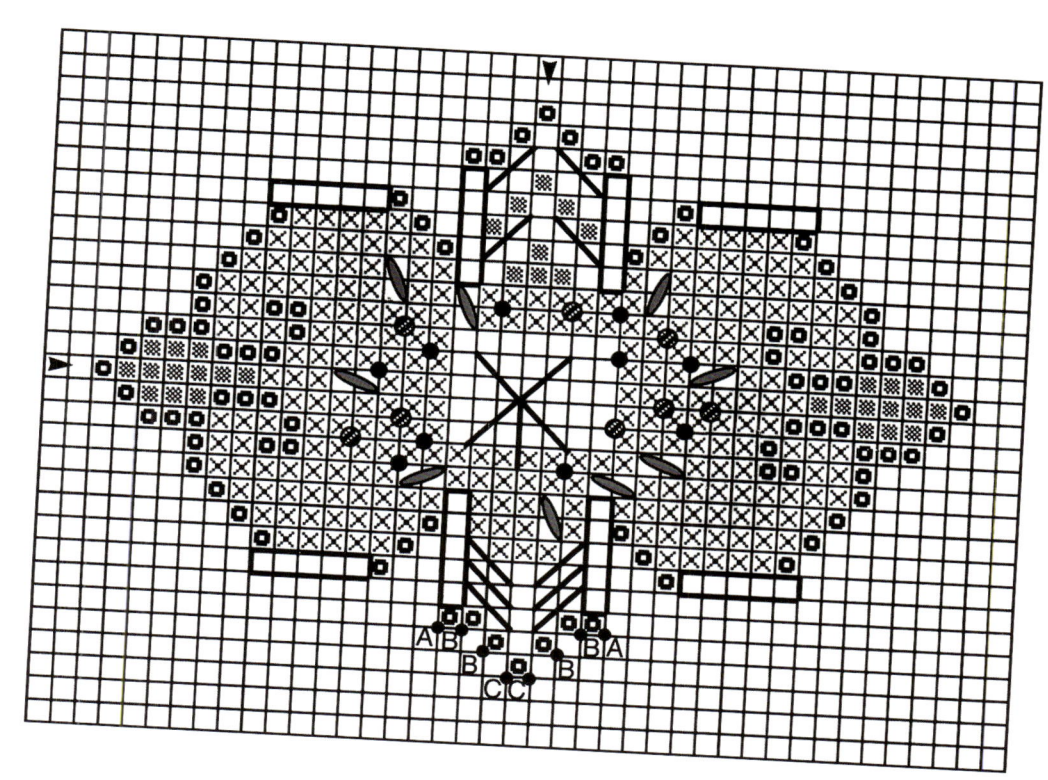

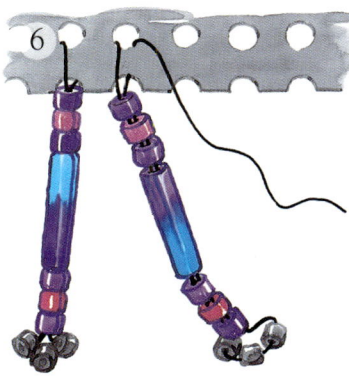

6 To make the fringe, attach five groups of beads at the bottom of the brooch. Thread three purple rocaille beads, one bugle, and three purple and three black rocaille beads on the needle. Return through these beads, starting with the fourth bead, forming a three-bead picot at the base of the fringe (see fig. 6).

KEY FOR TEMPLATE

stranded embroidery floss
- ✗ black
- ✖ lavender

ribbon
- ● ombre (blended) rose/purple
- ✗ purple
- ⬬ green

beads
- ◌ iridescent black (with black floss)
- ● plum (loops with lavender floss)
- ✻ dark purple (with black floss)
- ╱ small iridescent black bugle (with black floss)
- ▭ large iridescent black bugle (with black floss)

Variations
- For a change of color scheme, study a book on Art Deco jewelry and use the greens, reds, and golds that were popular during the 1930s.
- Use this idea to make an accessory to match a wedding or evening dress.
- Elongate the fringe or add more bead fringes to the bottom edge for a more dramatic effect.

EMBELLISHED EMBROIDERY KIT

Patchwork and Appliqué Pillowcase

In this pillowcase, the crisp effect of stripes is complemented by soft lace and romantic hearts, resulting in a fresh, pretty look for a bedroom. Appliqué and pieced borders are excellent ways to enliven solid colors, and the embroidery stitches chosen for this pillowcase will stand up to frequent washing.

MATERIALS AND EQUIPMENT

- **White cotton fabric 32 x 44 inches/82 x 110 cm**
- **Blue striped fabric 12 x 36 inches/28 x 90 cm**
- **Medium-weight iron-on interfacing**
- **2-inch-/5-cm-wide cotton lace edging 44 inches/110 cm long**
- **3/8-inch/1-cm-wide blue taffeta ribbon 44 inches/110 cm long**
- **Stranded embroidery floss in white, dark blue, and light blue**
- **White sewing thread**
- **Crewel embroidery needle**
- **Basic sewing equipment**
- **Template (see page 45)**

1

1 Cut one large heart and two small hearts from the interfacing, marking the large heart with a vertical arrow and the small hearts with horizontal arrows. Place the hearts, rough side down, on the striped fabric, aligning the arrows with the stripes and allowing plenty of space around each one. Iron to bond the fabrics (see fig. 1).

PATCHWORK AND APPLIQUE PILLOWCASE

2 Cut out the hearts with a ¼-inch/5-mm seam allowance. Clip the curves to within ⅛ inch/3 mm of the interfacing and the inner corner up to the interfacing. Fold and baste (tack) the fabric margin over the edge of the interfacing, starting with the knot on the right side. Trim excess fabric.

3

3 Cut a rectangle for the front, 22 x 20 inches/ 54.5 x 52 cm. Fold in half perpendicular to the shorter measurement; press lightly to mark the center. Baste (tack), and slipstitch the large heart at the center, 3½ inches/8 cm from the top, and the two smaller hearts 2 inches/5 cm to either side of the large one (see fig. 3). Remove all basting stitches. Using the crewel needle and three strands of dark blue floss, cover the edge of each heart using buttonhole stitch (see page 14). Finish with a row of feather stitch (see page 14), using three strands of light blue floss, around each motif.

Tips
- Always wash and iron new cotton fabrics before cutting them out.
- For a crisp finish, press the seams as you go.

4 For the patchwork borders, cut ten rectangles of striped fabric 5¾ x 5 inches/ 15 x 12.5 cm. Cut six with the short edges parallel to the stripes and four with the long edges parallel to the stripes.

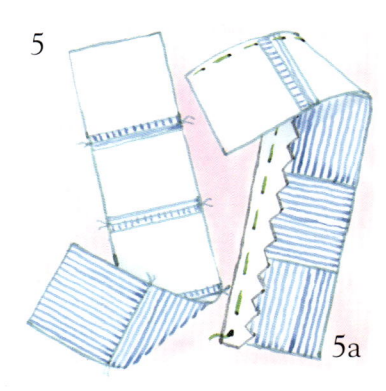

5

5a

5 Stitch the striped rectangles together along the longer edges in two groups of five, alternating the direction of the stripes (see fig. 5). Press the seams open. Baste (tack) the lace edging along one long edge of each patchwork strip, with the wrong side of the edging next to the right side of the fabric (see fig. 5a).

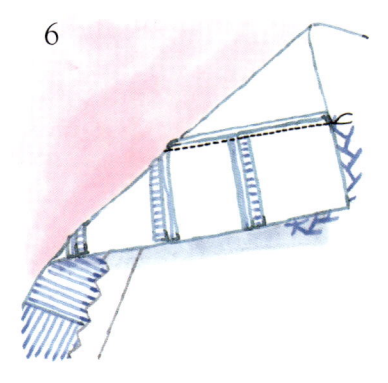

6

6 Stitch the lace edges of the strips to the longer edges of the front piece (see fig. 6).

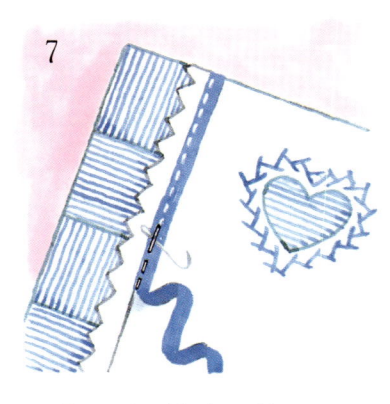

7

7 Baste (tack) the ribbon to the front, to cover the seams (see fig. 7). Using three strands of floss and running stitch, sew the ribbon along each edge. Work a row of light blue feather stitch parallel to the ribbon.

8 Cut one rectangle of white fabric 31¾ x 22 inches/ 81 x 54.5 cm for the back and one 22 x 8 inches/54.5 x 20 cm for the flap. Stitch a 1⅝-inch/ 4-cm hem on one short edge of the back and a ¼-inch/ 5-mm hem on a long edge of the flap.

9 Pin and stitch the flap to one short edge of the front, placing right sides together and matching raw edges. Press flat, still with right sides together.

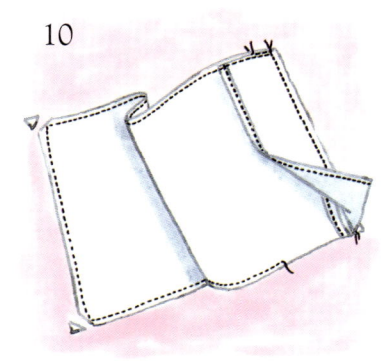

10

10 Open out the flap. Place the back on the front with right sides facing and the hemmed edge along the seam that joins the flap. Fold the flap back over the back. Pin and stitch through all three layers, around three sides, excluding the opening end; reinforce the stitching at the start and end points. Trim corners diagonally (see fig. 10). Press and turn the pillowcase right side out.

Variations
- Use printed ribbon and ready-gathered lace instead of the flat lace and plain ribbon.
- Use fabrics printed with small flowers and do the patchwork borders in pastel shades.

37

EMBELLISHED EMBROIDERY KIT

Autumn Sampler

Samplers are among the most familiar and valued of all old embroideries. Nowadays, they are stitched as pieces to commemorate family events or simply to complement an interior design scheme. This sampler, which features cross stitch, satin stitch and herringbone stitch, reflects the muted shades of late autumn.

MATERIALS AND EQUIPMENT

- **25-count beige linen 18 x 14 inches/46 x 36 cm**
- **Stranded embroidery floss in dark gray, dark blue, gray, plum, dark plum, and light gray**
- **Small rocaille beads in purple, copper, blackberry, dark copper, and dark gray.**
- **Small squirrel motif and four leaf-shaped motifs.**
- **Stretcher frame 14 x 11 inches/36 x 28 cm**
- **Tapestry needle**
- **Basic sewing equipment**
- **Template (see page 47 & 48)**

1 Fold the linen in half from top to bottom and run a line of basting (tacking) stitches along the fold to mark the center line. Press the fabric and mount in a frame.

2 Following the symbols on the chart and referring to the color key, work cross stitch (see page 13) in two strands of embroidery floss where thread (as opposed to bead) colors are specified. Add your own initials and the date.

3 Attach the beads with a half cross stitch over two intersections (see page 13), following the color symbols for beads on the chart.

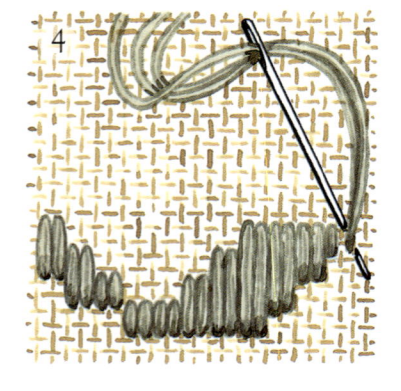

4 The satin stitch band is worked with a series of vertical stitches in three strands of gray floss, starting each stitch at the bottom (see fig. 4).

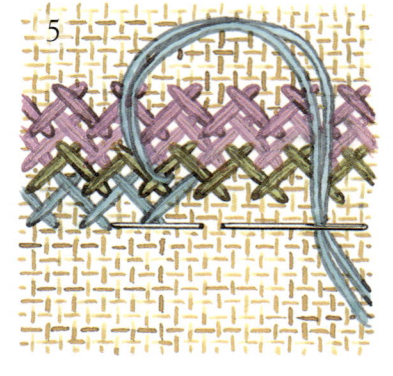

5 For the herringbone band, work six rows of herringbone stitch (see page 13); use two strands of floss for each in plum, dark plum, dark gray, dark blue, dark plum, and plum. First, work a row of herringbone stitch, with the diagonal stitches over four intersections of the evenweave fabric. Work the second row from left to right immediately below with the stitches encroaching halfway up the first row (see fig. 5).

AUTUMN SAMPLER

6 Sew or glue the squirrel and the leaf motifs in place.

Tips
- Keep an even tension when stitching so that the stitches lie smoothly on the surface without pulling the threads of the linen.
- Make sure that all the beads and cross stitches lie in the same direction.
- Take the finished piece to a professional framer who specilizes in mounting and framing textiles.
- Choose a mat (mount) and frame that complements the coloring of the sampler.

Variations
- Use this autumn sampler as inspiration for other projects depicting the seasons. To design your own, use this design as a starting point and work out your ideas on graph paper. For example, for a spring sampler, add blossom to the trees, embroider spring flowers such as primroses, and change the color of the background fabric.

EMBELLISHED EMBROIDERY KIT

Gallery

The traditional craft of embroidery is ever changing, and innovative designers are always experimenting with shapes and colors, textures and materials to produce unique and beautiful objects. This inspirational gallery shows just a few of the projects that have been made using this absorbing and interesting technique.

Pauline Brown A book in a slipcase

A small book with a woven gold kid suede front cover with designs embroidered in metal thread. The book sits in its own tailor-made case.

Mary Jo Hiney Designs Autumn brooch

A brooch worked in autumnal colors of paprika, moss and gold. It is enhanced with ribbon flowers, beading, crystal leaves, antique lace and tiny motifs.

MIXED MEDIA EMBROIDERY

Rachel Griffin Hearts and flowers: Ivory towers

Tiny pearl buttons, sequins, ribbon roses, motifs, beads, embroidery stitches, lace motifs and even postage stamps embellish this decorative picture.

41

EMBELLISHED EMBROIDERY KIT

Diana Dolman Lapis Lazuli

This beautiful fan is richly embroidered with gold and brilliant blue threads, and embellished with sparkling gold beads and blue beads.

Mary Jo Hiney Designs

Springtime sampler

This sampler is embellished with a variety of embroidered ribbon applications that are enhanced with silk floss, buttons, beads, vintage lace, crystal charms and tiny birds and rabbits.

Deirdre Hawken

Jester's Cap and Vest

Old ribbon, metal gauzes and lace, tarnished beads, brocade, pearls, thin copper sheet, and sequins are attached to a silk foundation. Buttons, beads and shells have been applied to a classic-shaped vest (right).

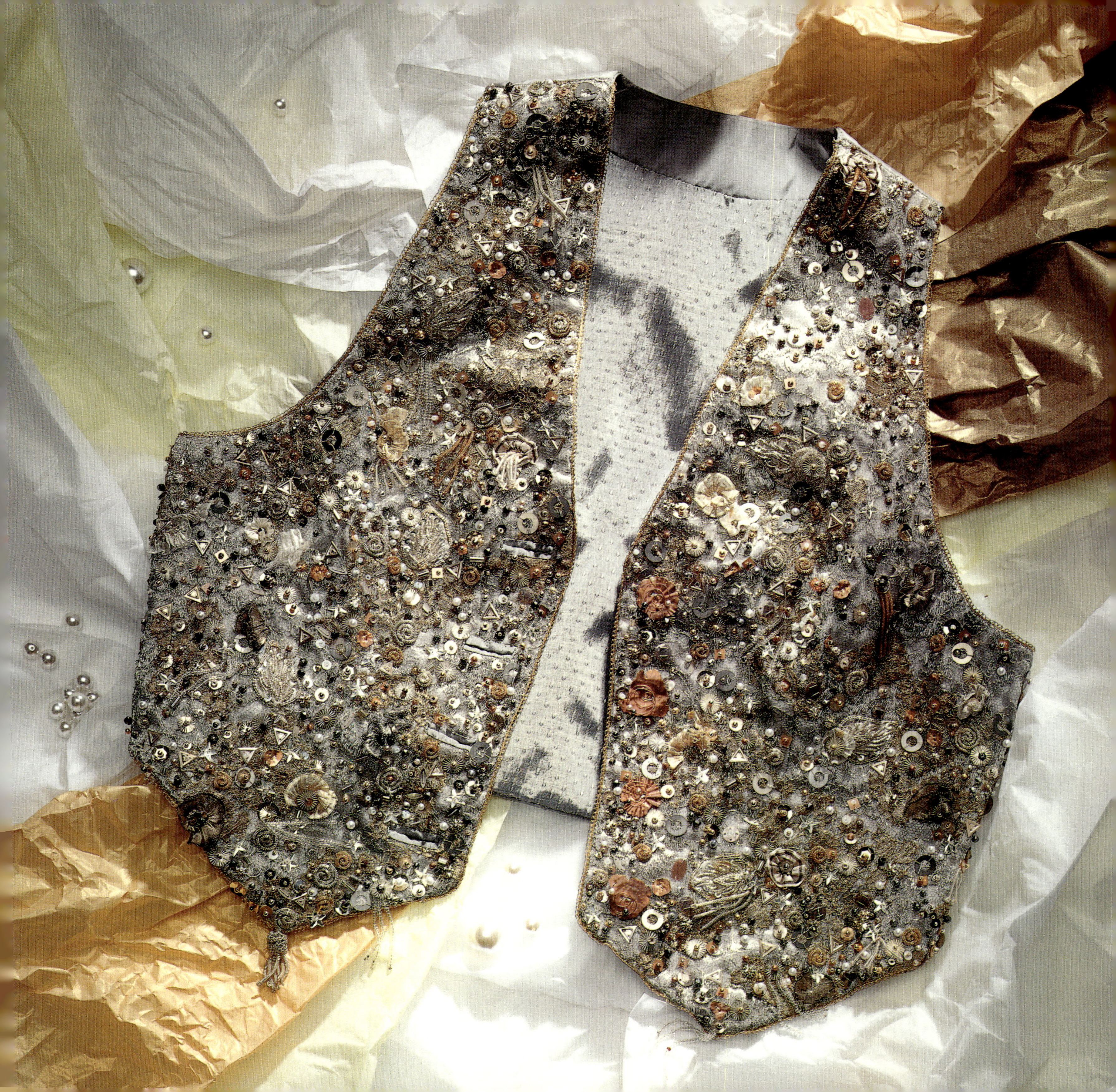

EMBELLISHED EMBROIDERY KIT

Templates

The templates shown can be used as a guide when transferring the designs to the fabric or canvas. Not all of the templates are full-size. Just enlarge as required.

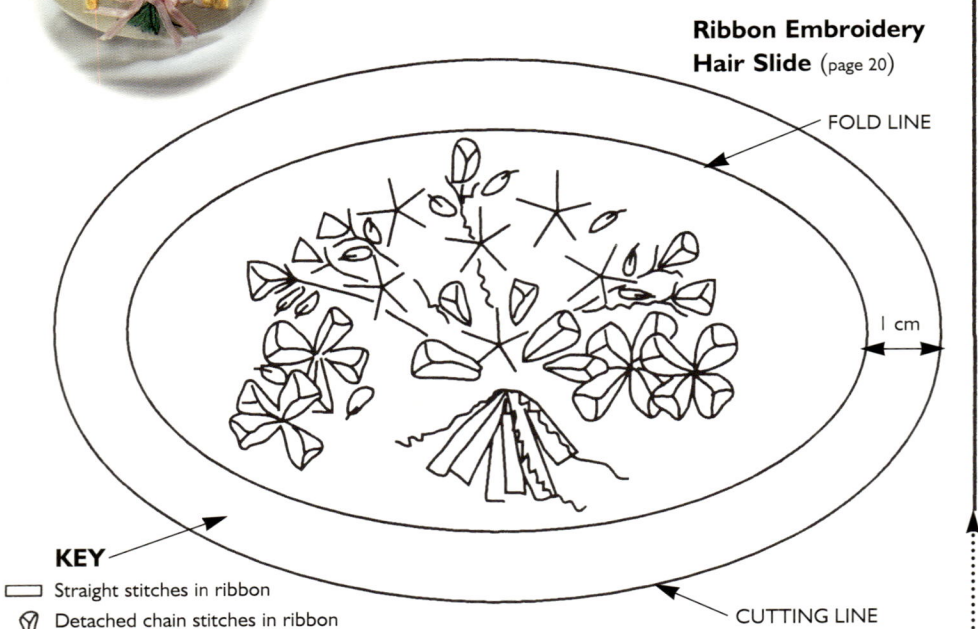

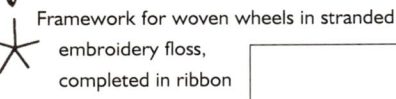

Ribbon Embroidery Hair Slide (page 20)

FOLD LINE

1 cm

CUTTING LINE

KEY
- Straight stitches in ribbon
- Detached chain stitches in ribbon
- Framework for woven wheels in stranded embroidery floss, completed in ribbon
- Fly stitch in embroidery floss
- Detached chain stitches in embroidery floss
- Stem stitch in embroidery floss

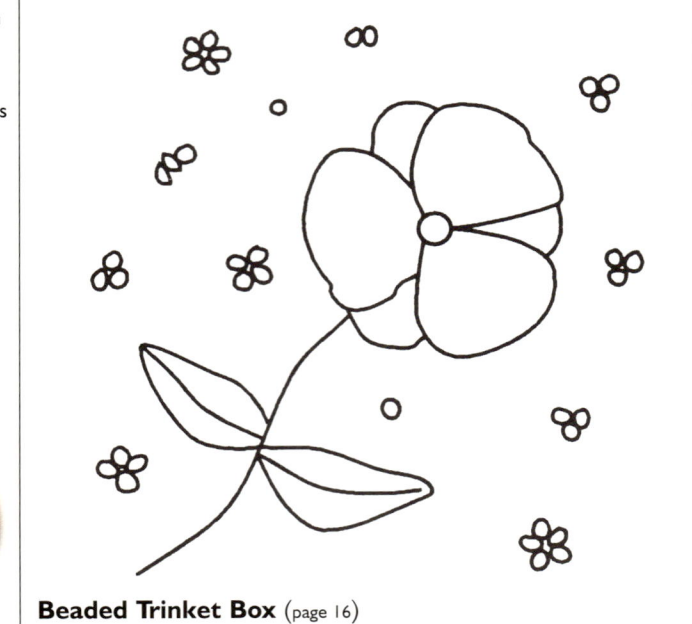

Beaded Trinket Box (page 16)

95 mm

95 mm

Elegant Evening Bag (page 18)

TEMPLATES

Wildflower Party Bolero (page 30)

FRONT
Cut 2 in velvet and in lining

BACK
Cut 1 on fold in velvet and in lining

FOLD LINE

Patchwork and Appliqué Pillowcase (page 36)

LARGE HEART

SMALL HEART

Cut 1 large and 2 small hearts in iron on interfacing

Appliqué Folk Art Picture (page 22)

Victorian Valentine Pincushion (page 26)

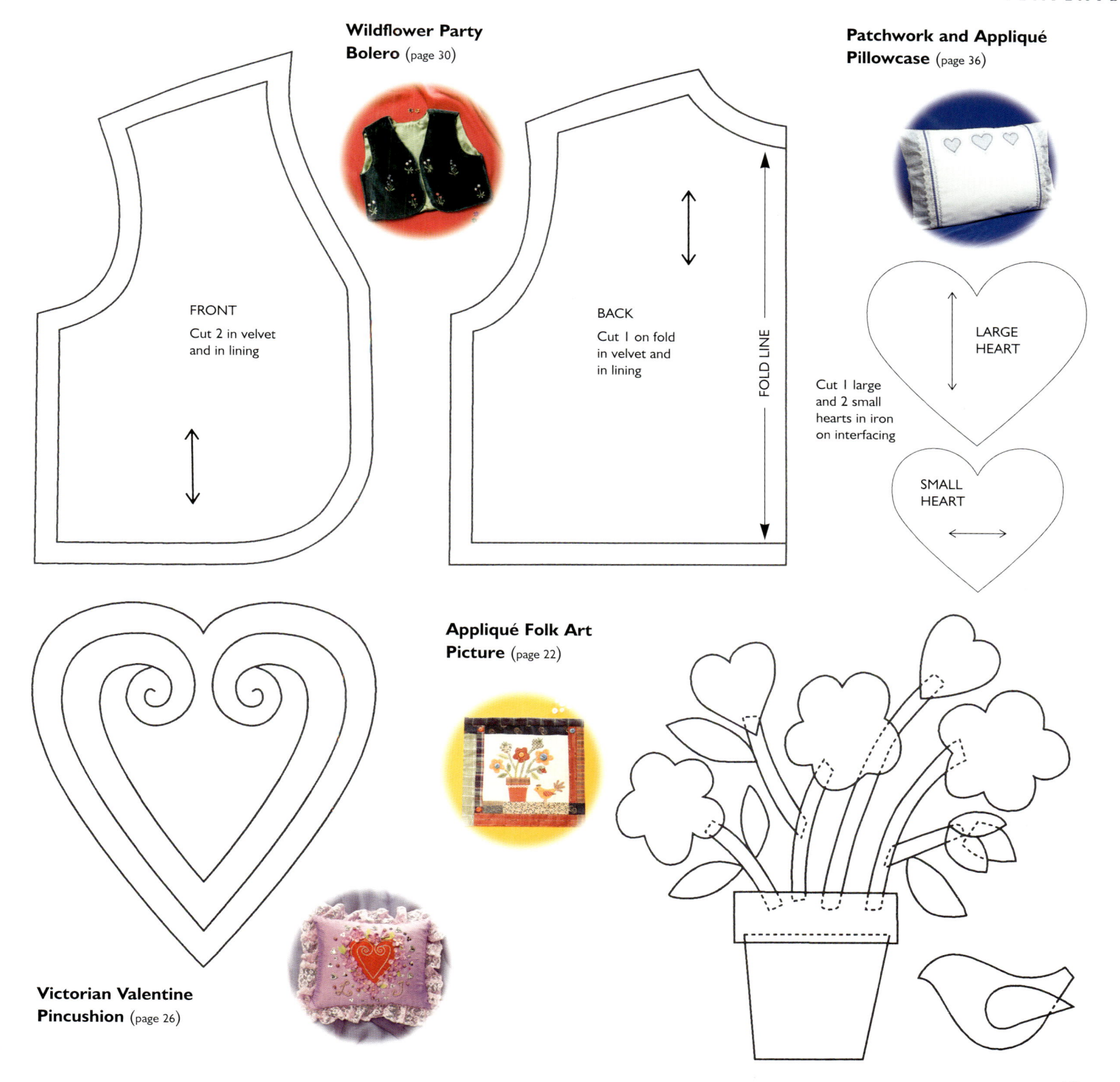

45

STARTING POINT

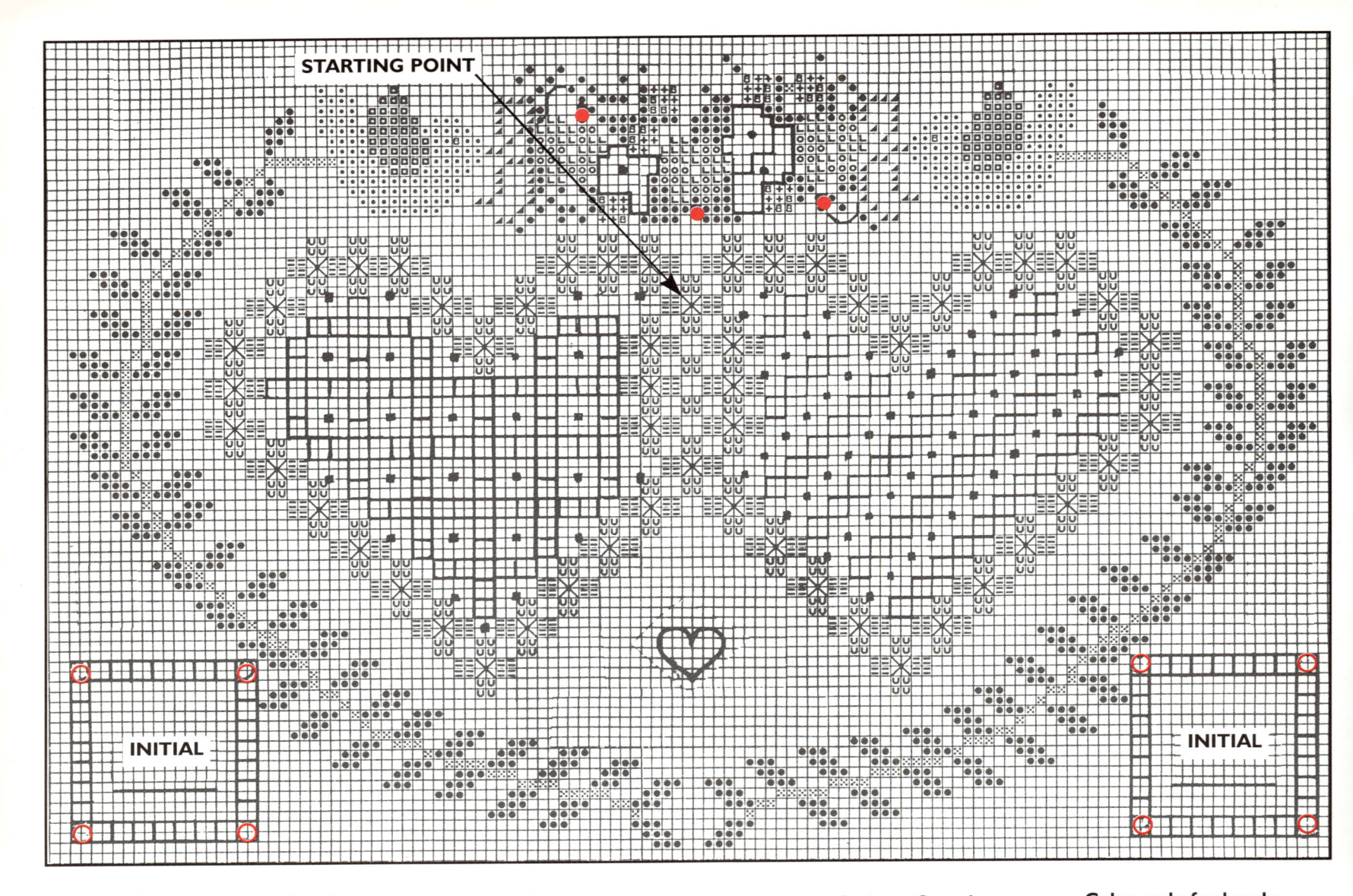

INITIAL

INITIAL

Wedding Ring Pillow (page 32)
Template shown at 100% size

KEY

embroidery threads:
- pale blue stranded floss
- pale green stranded floss
- T cream stranded floss
- synthetic gold metallic thread
- U & = cream pearl cotton No. 8

beads:
- pale green
- pale blue
- white pearl
- L pink
- dark pink
- B dark blue
- + blue

motifs:
- ● attach leaf motif
- ○ attach flower motif
- ♡ attach heart motif

Autumn Sampler (page 38)
Template shown right and continued on p.48 at 100% size

KEY

Color code for floss:
- dark gray
- dark blue
- gray
- plum, dark plum, light gray (for attaching beads)

Color code for beads:
- purple
- copper
- blackberry
- U dark copper
- dark gray

motifs:
- ■ attach leaf motif
- □ attach squirrel motif

46

SATIN STITCH BORDER

Continuation of Autumn Sampler template

HERRINGBONE VARIATION BORDER

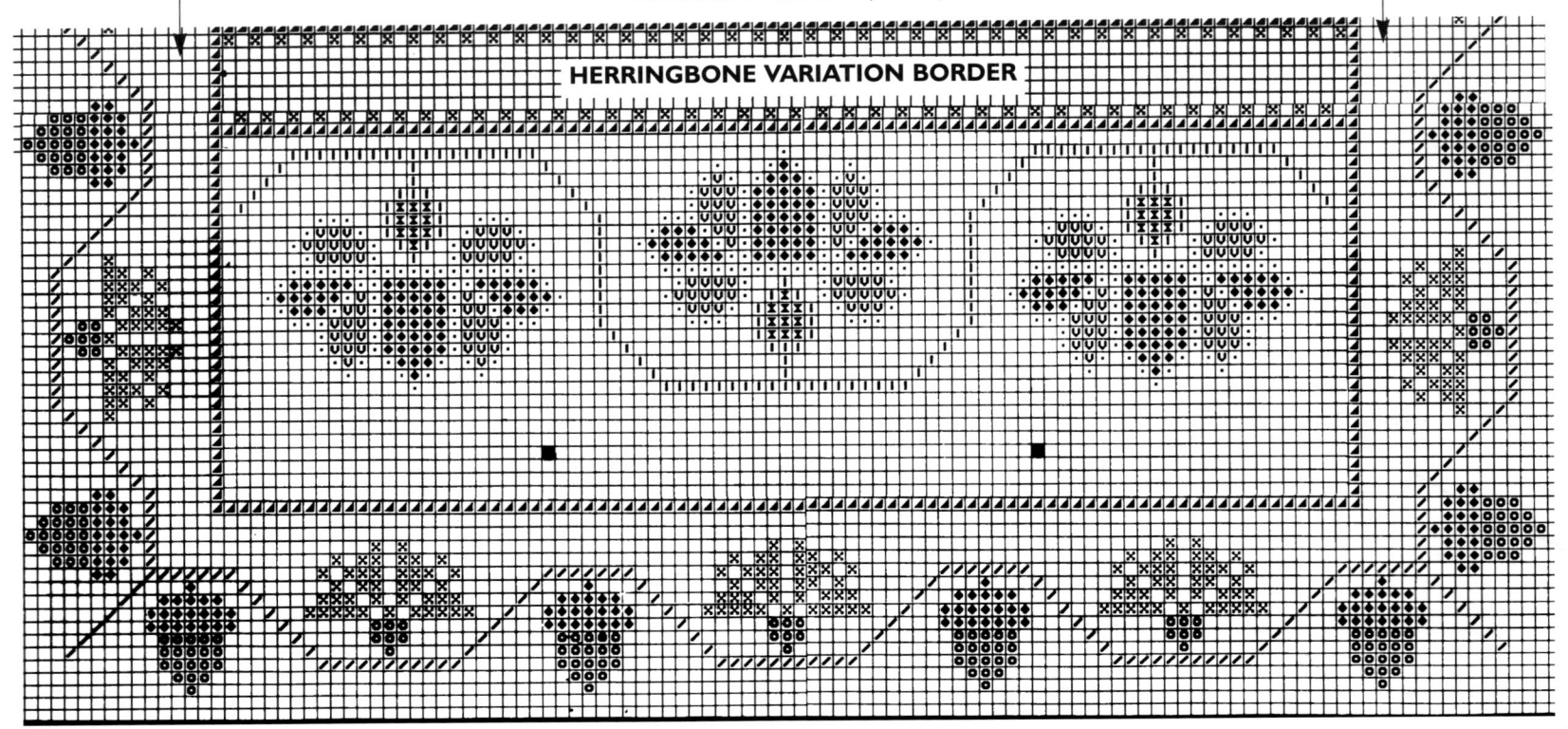

Index

A
Appliqué Folk Art Picture 22-3, 45
Art Deco Brooch 34-5
Autumn Brooch 40
Autumn Sampler 38-9, 47-8

B
backstitch 12
Beaded Trinket Box 16-17, 44
beads 9
Bolero, Wildflower Party 30-1, 45
Book in a slipcase 40
braid 9
braided cord 29
Brooch:
  Art Deco 34-5
  Autumn 40
Brown, Pauline 40
buttonhole stitch 14
buttons, covering 19

C
couching 14
cross stitch 13

D
design, transferring to fabric 10-11
Dolman, Diana 4, 42

E
Elegant Evening Bag 18-19, 44
embellishments 9
embroidery hoops 6
equipment 5-7
Evening Bag, Elegant 18-19, 44
Evening Purse, Sparkly 28-9

F
fabric markers 7, 10
fabrics 8
feather stitch 14
fly stitch 12
frames 6
French knots 14

G
Griffin, Rachel 41

H
Hair Slide, Ribbon Embroidery 20-1, 44
Hawken, Deirdre 42
Hearts and flowers: Ivory towers 41
herringbone stitch 13
Hiney, Mary Jo 40, 42
history 4
hoops 6

J
Jester's Cap and Vest 42-3
Jeweled Picture Frame 24-5
jewels, fake 9

K
kit components 15

L
lace edging 9
Lapis Lazuli 42
lazy daisy stitch 13

M
markers 7, 10
materials 8-9

N
needles 5

P
Patchwork and Appliqué Pillowcase 36-7, 45
Picture, Appliqué Folk Art 22-3, 45
Picture Frame, Jeweled 24-5
Pillowcase, Patchwork and Appliqué 36-7, 45
Pincushion, Victorian Valentine 26-7, 45

R
Ribbon Embroidery Hair Slide 20-1, 44
ribbons 9

S
Sampler:
  Autumn 38-9, 46-7
  Springtime 42
satin stitch 13
seed stitch 12
sequins 9
slipstitch 12
Sparkly Evening Purse 28-9
Springtime sampler 42

stem stitch 14
stitches 12-14
stretcher frames 6

T
templates 44-7
threads 8
tracing 11
trimmings 9
Trinket Box, Beaded 16-17, 44

V
Victorian Valentine Pincushion 26-7, 45

W
Wedding Ring Pillow 32-3, 46
Wildflower Party Bolero 30-1, 45